The Spirit Within

Created by

Antoinette Pellegrini

Book 4: We Inspire Now Series

First published by We Inspire Now Books 2023

Copyright © 2023 Antoinette Pellegrini

ISBN
Print: 978-0-6453052-3-4
Ebook: 978-0-6453052-4-1

Antoinette Pellegrini has asserted her right under the Copyright Act 1968 to be identified as the author of this work. The information in this book is based on each author's experiences and opinions. Each author retains copyright over their individual work.

Antoinette Pellegrini, as publisher through her business, We Inspire Now Books, specifically disclaims responsibility for any adverse consequences, which may result from use of the information contained herein in the works by the other individual authors. Each individual author takes responsibility for their content and for any permissions to use information. Any breaches will be rectified in future editions of the book.

This work is copyright. Apart from any use permitted under the Copyright Act 1968, no part of this publication may be reproduced, stored in or introduced into a retrieval system, or transmitted in any form, or by any means (electronic, mechanical, photocopying, recording or otherwise) without the prior written permission of the author. Any person who does any unauthorised act in relation to this publication may be liable to criminal prosecution and civil claims for damages. Enquiries should be made through the publisher.

Cover photograph and design: Antoinette Pellegrini

Layout and typesetting: Antoinette Pellegrini
                                We Inspire Now Books

We Inspire Now Books
PO BOX 133 Greensborough,
Victoria Australia 3088
www.weinspirenowbooks.com

Dedication

To my wonderful sons, Andrew and Robert, and to all of my friends and family who have inspired me to fulfil my dreams.

May you all follow your own dreams, live your passion, and be true to who you are, just as you have encouraged me to do.

Let your spirit within shine.

The first three books in the *We Inspire Now Anthology Series* were award-winning finalists at the International Book Awards at the American Book Fests.

Book 1:   *Live Your Truth* (2019 Awards)

Book 2:   *A Message To Your Younger Self: What Would You Say?* (2021 Awards)

Book 3:   *Journey To Me: A Discovery of Self* (2022 Awards)

Contents

Introduction	*Antoinette Pellegrini*	1
Awakening To Me	*Antoinette Pellegrini*	9
The Language of the Spirit: How Music Heals Us	*Andrea Sherko*	29
Keep Going	*Rosalie Carr*	39
Oh The Places You'll Go	*Christine Carmuciano*	53
Life in Pieces Through Dreams	*Dawn Sulley*	73
The Path(s) To Enlightenment	*Stephen D'Agata*	81
Still	*Liz Reichard*	97
An Unexplained Knowing	*Lesley Lennon*	109
Our Messages		131
Author Bios		143

Introduction

Antoinette Pellegrini

This book is the fourth book in the *We Inspire Now* Anthology Series.

The series featured a book exploring how to live your inner truth; another book explored what we would say to our younger selves, and more recently, authors wrote about the journey to becoming more themselves. This book, *The Spirit Within*, is the culmination of the previous three books, and explores our inner world.

What is 'the spirit within'?

There is no single answer to that question. It can be so many things, and not only do people have their own interpretations, but it can also mean different things to the one person.

The Inner Drive

For me, it has multiple meanings. First, it is the inner drive, the life force, that gets me up in the morning and helps me to keep going, despite the challenges life sometimes brings, and life has brought me many challenges. These have included bringing up two young sons on my own, dealing with the financial difficulties that come with being a single mother, the breakdown of subsequent relationships, and coping with negative, limiting beliefs about myself. Occasionally, I have woken up in the morning, feeling like I just wanted to stay in bed and avoid the world, but those days were very few, because there was a drive within me, saying, 'Get up and get going. There are so many things that are good in my life and so many things to look forward to.'

Purpose

The spirit within me is also the passion and purpose I feel, my 'why' for living – the things that make my heart sing. I find my purpose in being there for my sons, and also in my books, my message that 'Your Thoughts Matter', and in helping others to make their own voice heard.

For others, their 'why' may be their family, their work, or their creative talent, whether that be music, art, photography, research or invention. There are too many to mention, but whatever that 'why' is for you, it is your purpose, the spirit within.

Introduction

In my first book, *Your Thoughts Matter: The Future You Are Creating Starts Now*, I included a reflection entitled *Purpose*. I would like to share some of it here:

You were born for a reason.

You were born to experience life, to explore and be who you are - to make a difference. Life is an adventure we undertake. It is a journey.

Following our purpose is like forging your own trail upon the Earth. It means making your own path and not simply following what others do. Your life is your journey. No one before, or after you, will have the same journey. You are unique.

Purpose gives meaning to our lives. It makes us go beyond the everyday. When you are driven by a sense of purpose and meaning, you can tolerate almost anything.

Victor Frankl, a doctor, psychologist and survivor of the Auschwitz concentration camp, wrote about his experiences and his theory that the primary motivation for man is the search for a meaning to life. He stated that it is only through having a sense of purpose and meaning to life that we can survive hardship and suffering and quoted Nietzsche who stated that "He who has a why to live can bear almost any how"[1]. *Frankl discovered that even in the horrific conditions of the concentration camp, it was the people who had a sense of purpose and meaning and a goal to strive for, who were the most likely to survive.*

---

[1] Frankl, Viktor, E., *Man's Search For Meaning*, Pocket Books, New York, 1984, page 97.

Having a sense of purpose and meaning is vital to us. Most of us will never have to endure the devastating conditions of a concentration camp, but even in our lives, if we live without a sense of purpose, our existence may seem like an endless repetition of the same everyday tasks.

Without a sense of purpose, life can seem empty - but everyone has a purpose. No-one's life is empty and meaningless. We all make a difference. Your life and your purpose is unique to you – it is yours alone. There is no right or wrong. What brings meaning to your life is different from what brings meaning to others. What brings meaning to you can, and probably will change, throughout your life. The challenge is to be yourself, to forge your own path along your journey.

You may be driven to do something in particular. This is the feeling at the core of your being that there is something you have to do in life. It is the feeling that something is missing. Until you find out what it is and complete it, your life's experience does not seem complete. For many, their purpose is to simply survive, for some it is to have children, others may be driven to devote their lives to other people. No choice is better or worse than another. There is only what is right for you and only you will know that.

Whatever you are here to do, you will know if you have achieved it by listening to your feelings. Do you feel fulfilled and happy with your life or do you have the feeling deep down that something is missing, that there is something you have left undone?

To find your purpose, follow your heart. What are your true feelings? Where do they lead you? What gives you joy? What would you do if you didn't have to worry about money and had the time and energy to do whatever you want? Your purpose is that which fulfills you.

We all have things we feel we must do that stop us from doing what we want to do. But is it really all or nothing? Can you find a way to live your dreams? They are a key to your purpose, a key to your soul – to who you really are.[2]

Everyone has a different 'why'. It could be a passion, it could be family, but ultimately, perhaps our purpose, our 'why' is to be fully who we are. To be ourselves and live in a way that is true to who we are.

One of my favourite quotes is:

Do not go where the path may lead,
go instead where there is no path and leave a trail.
Ralph Waldo Emerson (1803 – 1882)

Connection

We are all unique, and if we are truly ourselves, and true to our spirit within, then we will forge our own path – there is no need to copy anyone else.

The 'why', the spirit within, is a powerful force, but I believe it is even more than that. I believe that the

---

[2] Pellegrini, Antoinette, *Your Thoughts Matter: The Future You Are Creating Starts Now*, Busybird Publishing, 2017, Chapter 18: *Purpose*, pp 107-109

spirit within me also connects me to everything and everyone else.

My belief that we are vibrations of energy consciousness is a belief supported by quantum physics, which states that all matter, indeed everything in the universe, is a vibration of energy. We are vibrations of energy; not just our physical bodies, but our thoughts and feelings are energy vibrations, affecting not only our health and wellbeing but affecting those around us as well. My consciousness, the spirit within me, is a vibration that is me, and perhaps it really is the whole of me. And my energy vibration, my spirit, is not separate from the universal energy that makes up everything else in existence. We are all part of the whole.

Who You Are

Ultimately, I believe that the spirit within is actually who you are. Science tells us that we are vibrations of energy consciousness. That is what I call spirit. So perhaps 'the spirit within' is not quite the right phrase. Perhaps, it should just be, 'The Spirit', because it is the whole of who we are.

The 'magic' happens when you are in alignment with the spirit within, when your everyday life, actions, choices, feelings, and thoughts align with your inner passion, drive, and spirit. Perhaps this is a description of happiness: when everything is in alignment, and you feel totally at peace with who you are. When your inner spirit matches the external circumstances of your life, then you are truly living the manifestation of who you are. This isn't always easy.

Sometimes, external circumstances force us to look within. The death of my mother during the Covid-19 pandemic lockdown in Melbourne, was such a moment for me. My father passed away many years before, so with the death of my mother, I was an orphan at the age of 60.

I acutely felt my mortality, and had the realisation that life is indeed too short, and that our days on Earth are numbered. What was important to me was to truly live the days that are left to me – to be true to myself and the spirit within me, so that I truly fulfil my 'why', my passion and my purpose, and to be true to myself.

The Covid 19 pandemic has done that for many people. The difficulties, lockdowns, separation from family and friends and the deaths of many, forced people to re-evaluate their lives, and search within for what really makes them happy.

The authors in this book have all gone on their own journey to find the spirit within, and it means different things to each of them. For some, it is the inner drive, the life force that gets you up in the morning and helps you to keep going, despite the challenges life sometimes brings. For others it is their music, or reconciling their beliefs and their religion. It can be deeply spiritual, involving experiences that some would describe as 'beyond normal'. Or it may be finding passion and purpose, but perhaps for all, it's about getting in touch with their core, who they are deep within.

I imagine that some of the stories will resonate with you more than others. I hope that our stories will encourage and inspire you to look within, to find your own spirit within, and honour whatever it is that makes your heart sing.

Awakening To Me

Antoinette Pellegrini

Your spirit within is your gift to yourself and to the world.
Let your spirit sing!

Antoinette Pellegrini

It was 1987, and I was sitting cross-legged on the floor in a circle of mostly women, strangers except for my sister and a friend. It was a workshop on crystals and chakras, but I had very little understanding of what either of these were. The facilitator asked us to share the reason we were there, and luckily, she started with the person to her left, which gave me some time to think of a suitable answer. I didn't think I should tell her the real reason – that I had finally given in to my sister's constant requests for me to go to one of the spiritual workshops she regularly attended.

My younger sister had been exploring spirituality for a few years. She was a healer and popular with her clients. I was a sceptic. More than that – for most of my life I had been an atheist.

It didn't start that way. I was born into an Italian family and was, therefore, Catholic. I went to Catholic schools and, in my early years, went regularly to church. But by 14 years of age, I was starting to question the church and religion. It began with my observation of some priests and nuns at school and church. I saw men and women who were angry, opinionated and thought they were superior to us 'mere mortals'. I didn't feel they lived by the Christian values they were teaching us. I thought they were hypocrites.

I started to question religion. Why were there so many different religions? Why did they all think they were right? Why did they think that their way was the only way to salvation and that every person who followed another religion was doomed? Why were so many wars fought over religion? Why were there so many rules that didn't make sense? Why couldn't we eat meat on a Friday? I remember challenging my mother about this, 'Why would the God who made the entire universe and all the amazing things in it, care if we ate meat on a Friday?' Mum didn't have an answer. I concluded that religion was a man-made construct designed to control people.

I questioned God as well – especially the God in the Old Testament, who seemed to be angry, vengeful, and unforgiving. Why should I look up to that God? Outwardly, I was still the 'good Catholic girl'. I went to church and to Catholic school, but inwardly, I was a rebel.

By 15, I had rejected it all. I believed we were born, live and die – that's it. I was an atheist. No one was going to change my mind.

In my early twenties, I was engaged to be married and didn't want to get married in a church. This devastated my parents. My father arranged for a priest to come and talk to me to convince me that I needed to get married in a church. All that happened was a thrilling hour-and-a-half discussion on religion and the existence of God. Every argument the priest came up with, I had a counter-argument. The priest finally ended our conversation by saying, 'Well, I guess it is a matter of faith' and walked out of our house.

I am sure that priest thought I would burn in hell. I think my parents thought that too. He hadn't convinced me about the existence of God, but to appease my parents, I did concede to get married in a church. However, I insisted it be in a Uniting Church, a compromise that made my parents happy and satisfied me to the extent that it seemed to be a more liberal church than the Catholic Church I grew up with. After all, I didn't want my parents to be unhappy at my wedding.

Although I had rejected the church and the existence of God, the one thing I didn't reject was the teachings of Jesus. I didn't see him as the 'son of God', but I did see him as a prophet, a teacher, and I tried to live my life according to his teachings – 'love one another as yourself', 'do unto others as you want them to do unto you', and to forgive, 'turn the other cheek'. I used to think, 'If only Christians and others followed his teachings, the world would be a much better place.'

Over the years, my position as an atheist did change slightly. As I got older, I recognised that perhaps I didn't know for sure about how the universe worked. I became agnostic. My younger sister had discovered spirituality and often spoke to me about it. I found it a different way of looking at the world. It was not about obeying rules and fearing punishment, but one of inclusiveness and personal responsibility. I liked the concepts but was still very sceptical. My sister consistently asked me to come along to the workshops she attended. I resisted for years until finally, at about age 36, I agreed.

So, that is how I found myself at a chakra and crystal workshop with my sister. The facilitator asked everyone why they were there and what they were hoping to achieve from the workshop. It was nearly my turn to tell the group why I was there. What should I say? I didn't know what I wanted from the workshop.

It was finally my turn, and I was about to speak when IT happened; an AWAKENING – literally.

Before I had a chance to say anything, I felt a blow to the top of my head. I visibly flinched, and I heard the words, 'Wake up!'. It was like an exasperated teacher had slammed a book onto the head of a reluctant student who was nodding off or not paying attention. I opened my mouth to speak, and the words that came out of my mouth were, 'I have a job to do, and I need to find out what it is.' The facilitator nodded, accepted my answer and moved on to the next person.

I, on the other hand, was in shock and disbelief. What had just happened? Who or what had hit me? Who said the words, 'Wake up!'? No-one was standing behind or in front of me. And what did I mean by what I said? Am I going insane? What job did I have to do? How do I find out?

I could barely sit still. My eyes, my mind and my spirit were opened that night. I learnt about energy, and I saw outlines of the etheric energy fields around some of the participants. I began to remember experiences I had as a child, when in prep, I would sit cross-legged on the floor at school, casually watching the auric field of my arms move in and out of my body.

Other experiences came flooding back that night. I remembered an incident when I was ten years old and had nearly drowned.

I had been walking in the ocean with my aunt. We had been walking together, chatting about nothing in particular. I was having fun; going to the beach was a rare occurrence when I was young. It was a beautiful sunny day; the water was cool, and the waves gentle, and I felt comfortable with the water reaching my chest.

Another step, and suddenly the seafloor gave way under my feet. I was under the water. I felt a moment of panic and then a total calm. I could see my face. I have heard that people who have had near-death experiences say that they remember looking down at their dying bodies. I can't say exactly what happened to me, but I do remember looking at myself.

I remember calmly watching myself drown. I was outside of my body and could see myself only a few feet in front of me, my eyes startled and wide open, my hair flowing upwards in the water, my arms flailing and my mouth wide open with bubbles escaping upwards, yet I was totally calm, detached and at peace.

I felt a little of that peace now. Yet this time, there was an expansive feeling, a feeling of connection, a feeling that there was much more to this world than the physical world we see around us.

I understood that this near-drowning incident had been a decision point. I had a choice at ten years of age to leave this Earth. I chose not to. Maybe my spirit knew of the difficulties and hardships ahead of me and was giving me a choice. I am very grateful to my ten-year-old self for having the courage to stay.

That night at the workshop was my awakening and the start of my spiritual journey, or perhaps a remembering of the journey that I had started as a little girl, a journey that I am still on. A journey to discover who I am, why I am here, what my purpose is, and to pursue the passion and drive inside me – to discover my spirit within.

I began reading spiritual books and joined spiritual groups. The first book I read was *The Body Is The Barometer of The Soul*, by Annette Noontil[3]. This book talked about our ailments and diseases having their basis in our thoughts and feelings. It opened my mind to new possibilities. I then came across the book, *Conversations With God, Book 1* by Neale Donald Walsch[4]; you could say, an unlikely book for an atheist to read. It represented a totally new way of seeing 'God' – not an entity separate from us, who sits in

---

[3] Noontil, Annette, *The Body Is The Barometer Of The Soul*, 1994, McPherson's Printing Group, Australia.
[4] Neale Donald Walsch, *Conversations with God: An Uncommon Dialogue Book 1*, Hodder Headline Australia, 1995

judgement, and controls through rules and punishments, but an all-encompassing conscious energy, that we are part of. In that book, God was '*All That Is*,'[5] and we were not separate from that energy; he was an accessible God. Finally, I had found a God that I could believe in. I needed to learn more.

I started meditating and learnt Reiki, an energy healing modality, eventually becoming a Reiki Master. Later, I was to study Holistic Counselling and Mind Body Medicine, but the sceptic was still inside me, and I needed proof that what I was starting to experience was real. I got the validation I needed again and again.

I was getting messages from people who had passed. At first it was for my parents. I got messages about their younger siblings who had passed at a very early age, only three or four. They were things I had never heard about or could have known. I got messages for others as well. At one of my groups, a woman was telling me that she was very close to her grandmother, but as she spoke, I kept getting the message that her grandmother died at age 28. That didn't make sense, but I finally told her, and she confirmed that that was, in fact, the case. She had never known her grandmother, but had always felt close to her.

Once I received a message from my ex-husband's grandfather who had passed. I asked for something that would be meaningful to my then-husband. I got the image of a little red wagon. This brought my

---

[5] Neale Donald Walsch, *Conversations with God: An Uncommon Dialogue Book 1*, Hodder Headline Australia, 1995, pages 22-26.

husband close to tears, as it had been his favourite toy. There is no way for me to have known that.

The validations came again and again. Every time I asked for proof, and I asked often, the proof came.

The most significant of these validations happened at a spiritual circle I attended on a Monday evening. The man who ran the group regularly channelled four entities who had passed. It was always the same four spirits, and I was always amazed that each had a very distinctive voice and energy. But of course, I now know that this is not surprising at all. We all have our own distinctive energy vibration, and that doesn't change after we pass and change form.

One particular night in 1999, I was running late, and whilst driving, I was talking with Jesus, the Christ energy. The way the conversation worked was that I would say something in my mind, and I would get a response that I knew wasn't me.

I talked with Jesus often as I had always felt close to him and his teachings, even when I was an atheist. Then the thought came to me, 'I must be out of my mind to think I am talking with Jesus.' The response came, 'You are, my child.' 'Prove it to me,' was my response. 'Come through to the channelling group tonight.' The response was, 'Yes, I will.'

I simultaneously felt like a Doubting Thomas and a crazy fool. Was I going mad? How could I think I was talking with Jesus? And if it was Jesus, I had just challenged him to prove it to me. Oh, God!!

Anyway, by then, I had arrived and rushed inside to take my seat in the circle. The session was about to start, so I couldn't say much more than 'Hello' to everyone. It started as usual; the first channelling, then the second, but then there was a noticeable energy shift, different from the energies usually channelled. The first words were, 'Greetings. It has been a long time since I have walked on the Earth.' It continued, but I could barely sit still. I knew it was Jesus. He had come through. The channelling ended by signing off as the Christ energy.

The channeller was shocked. He told us that he had never channelled the Christ energy before. That had been the first time. I could barely believe it. I had asked Jesus to come to the channelling group that night, and he did. I had asked for proof, and I got it. The session was taped, and I received a copy. I can still barely believe it.

I thought to myself, 'I have either gone completely crazy, or this is how the world is.' I didn't think I was crazy, and the validations I received were real, so I turned to science. If this is how the world is, then science needs to be able to explain it, or at least be consistent with what I had been experiencing. This took me to quantum physics.

What I discovered is that we are all energy, and that all matter is energy vibrating at a lower frequency. I discovered that energy doesn't die; it just changes form, similar to water which exists as a solid in ice, liquid, gas as steam, and invisible vapour in the air, as it rises to form clouds and falls again as rain. I discovered that at the quantum level, everything exists as a wave of possibilities, which becomes something when an observer is involved, even if they are just thinking about the outcome. In other words, we change the many possibilities that exist in our lives into our reality through our thoughts, feelings, choices and actions. I learnt that we are, therefore, the key creators of our lives, and we are not alone.

Everything is connected, or quantumly entangled, so we are affected by others. I learnt that everything that exists in our universe has its origins in the Big Bang, and that the elements that are in the stars, are in us too. I learnt that there is really only one universal energy, and we and everything in the universe are part of it. I learnt that the basis of all reality may indeed be thought or consciousness. All of this is what I learnt from quantum physics, and it was very similar, if not the same, as what I was learning and reading about in the spiritual books. I realised that physics and metaphysics were saying the same thing.

Everything was starting to make sense for me and coming together into a coherent whole. Spirituality wasn't something I believed; it was something I was, that we all are. I am the physical person, Antoinette Pellegrini, but I am also energy consciousness and individual 'soul' or 'spirit' that is also connected to everyone and everything in the universe, and that energy never dies. It therefore made sense that I could get messages from people who had passed, because they too were energy consciousness.

Science is still learning about consciousness and how it works. The power of thought is still being discovered. I realised that how we think matters. It is the basis that determines how we live. I understood that although we may not always be able to control what happens to us, we are always in control of how we respond to the circumstances of our lives, and we can choose to respond positively or negatively. That choice can literally change our physical bodies, as our thoughts release chemicals and hormones into our bodies, which can work for us or cause disease.

I knew that the job I needed to do was to tell people what I was discovering, but how do I do that? I still didn't know. The challenge for me was how to incorporate what I was learning into my life.

At the time I was discovering all of this, I was working in a corporate public sector job and I was in a second marriage that wasn't aligning with the new person I was becoming.

My first marriage had ended when my husband walked out, and I was left with bringing up a two-year-old and a three-month-old baby on my own. To say I was devastated was an understatement, and the difficulties of bringing up two young children as a sole parent were compounded by my feelings of unworthiness and loneliness.

A few years later, I met the man who would be my second husband. Our marriage lasted three years, but even before we were married, the universe, my gut, my intuition, my spirit within, was screaming at me that this was not right. I knew that he wasn't right for me, that it wasn't going to work, but I ignored it. The need for love and validation overrode my intuition.

One vivid example of this was when we were looking for an engagement ring. I was adamant that I wanted the ring to be different from my first engagement ring. We had looked in what seemed to be every jewellery store in Melbourne. Finally, I found a ring that I loved. I was thrilled with it until I got home.

I wanted to compare the rings, so I got my old engagement ring out. I put them side by side and just stared in disbelief. I had been determined that I wanted something totally different, yet the rings were identical except that my new one was bigger! It had the same intricate crossover design and the same diamond cut. I knew immediately that this was a message, a sign that this was not the right marriage for me, but I ignored it.

I ignored the fact that our interests, and, more importantly, our values were so different. He was into war games and mediaeval role-playing, and I was discovering spirituality and learning Reiki.

I remember an incident that shone a light, like a beacon, on our differences. One Sunday afternoon, he came to me very excited and proud of himself. 'I've created a website for us, come and have a look.' I followed him into the study, and on the front page of the website in huge letters was 'Contact us for War Games and Reiki'. I stared in disbelief. 'You can't have those two things together. Please take me and Reiki out of it.'

He was devastated and hurt, and although I tried to explain it to him, he didn't understand why I was upset. He didn't understand that those two things were diametrically opposed, and so were we. It was inevitable that the marriage would end.

I finally ended my marriage when I found out that he was having an affair. He said that it didn't mean anything to him, that he still loved me and wanted us to stay together, and perhaps that was true, however, I knew that we were too different, that what we wanted from life was very different, and I knew I had to end the marriage. You could say that our energies were not vibrating at a similar frequency. Perhaps they never were. I hadn't listened to my intuition at the beginning of our relationship, but I had changed over the three years we were married. I was becoming stronger, I was finding myself, discovering my inner strength, my spirit within, and I couldn't ignore my intuition anymore.

I had to start to live the new me that I was discovering. I had to discover what my 'job' was, what I was here to do.

The one thing I knew was that the job I was actually doing, wasn't the job I needed to do. Working in a corporate job in the public sector was becoming increasingly difficult. It wasn't aligning with what my spirit wanted to do, but I couldn't leave just yet. I was still a single mum and my sons were financially dependent on me.

I began to write. I had never thought of myself as a writer, but the inspiration came, often at the strangest times; at 3.00am when I should have been asleep or on the train on the way to work. I started carrying a notebook with me. The idea for books arose. I needed to publish, to share what I was discovering, but I had no idea how to do that. I trusted the universe would show me the way.

It wasn't always easy. There were difficulties along the way, and some expensive detours. I managed to publish an early version of my first book in 2006, but it wasn't what I had wanted. The publisher had taken it over. I didn't promote it and left the box of books at the bottom of my cupboard, where they still are. I promised myself that I would re-publish it the way I wanted. My spirit was determined, no matter how long I needed to wait.

It took another 11 years until I was ready; ready to leave my corporate job and focus on the work my spirit wanted me to do. I found a publisher I could trust, and published my first book, *Your Thoughts Matter,* in 2017. Then came the anthology series, called *We Inspire Now*. I hadn't intended to publish these stories, but again, the universe had other ideas.

It all started in October 2015, following a conversation with three of my girlfriends on a beach in Koh Samui, Thailand. It was a beautiful warm evening. The sun was setting over the water, changing the sky to hues of orange and yellow. The waves were lapping onto the shore, and we were enjoying watching the end of another idyllic day.

Our conversation flowed, and soon we found ourselves talking about menopause. We were all in our early to mid-fifties, so it was an obvious topic to talk about, even on the beach at sunset. Laughing and sipping cocktails, we compared notes about hot flushes, night sweats, our sex drives and relationships.

Then one of my friends became serious and said that she was dreading menopause because for her, it meant that she was an old crone, and that her life would no longer have purpose or meaning, and that it was all downhill from there.

I was shocked by this. I couldn't believe that she felt like that. For me, menopause was different. I was so happy and relieved not to have periods any more. Besides this, I felt that I was finally getting me back. It was my time to finally do what I wanted to do, and yet she felt the opposite.

I thought about menopause and considered why I felt so positive about it whilst others were not. Partly, the reason could be that I did not have severe issues with menopause. I did have hot flushes – often at the most inconvenient times, at work, on the train, and even at interviews! Night sweats were also a regular occurrence, throwing the sheets and doonas on and off for most of the night, nearly every night.

None of this mattered. I felt very positive about these symptoms, because they were bringing me closer to menopause. I would see advertisements for supplements to ease menopause symptoms, but I didn't want any of these. For me, it was a natural process, not a disease that had to be medicated. In saying this, I am not critical of women who need or want to ease their symptoms – everyone chooses for themselves.

As an Energy and Mindset Therapist, I knew that how you approach something in life, either from a positive or negative viewpoint, can have a significant impact on the outcome, physically, mentally and emotionally. Your thoughts matter. The way you think directly impacts on your health and wellbeing, even changing your body chemistry.

Was this the difference between how I felt and how my friend felt? Your mindset affects, indeed in a very real sense, creates your outcome.

I realised that menopause for me was a metaphor - a symbol that my life was not just about being a mother, although I would always be that. Menopause meant that for the first time since I was 12 years old, my body was now just for me and not just about giving to others. Menopause somehow gave me permission to finally concentrate on me, to do what I wanted and to finally fulfil my dreams.

That night I thought about what my friend had said and wondered how many other women feel that menopause and getting older means that they no longer have meaning or purpose.

I managed to get to sleep but woke up at 3 am and started writing. I felt driven to write a book to help inspire people to fulfil their dreams, to show them that it's not over in their 50s and it's never too late to pursue their passion; that it's never too late to go after what they want.

Like any idea, it morphed and changed, and by the time I was ready to write a year later, I realised that the book couldn't be just about women and menopause. I also realised that it couldn't be just me writing the book, that it needed to have other co-authors sharing their own inspirational stories of overcoming hardships and following their dreams - so the idea of the *We Inspire Now Anthology Series* was born.

After my second book, I was inspired to publish my own books, undertaking the whole publishing process from start to finish. People started approaching me to help them publish their books, so We Inspire Now Books publishing was born. I discovered how healing, cathartic, and even life-changing writing can be for the author, and how inspiring such writing is for the reader. The mission for my business became, 'Write to Heal, Publish to Inspire.' Is this the job I was meant to do? It is for now, and I am open to where the journey of my life will take me.

All I know is that the spirit within me sings when I write and when I help others share their story with the world, and that is the key to knowing that who I am and what I am doing is aligning; my spirit within is aligning with the universal spiritual energy that I am part of.

In 2022 I finally published my children's illustrated book *Sandcastles: A Story About Our Connected World*. It was something I had wanted to do for more than 20 years. Its message, that we are unique and yet connected to everything else was inspired by my belief in our connected world, a world of energy consciousness where physics and spirituality are one.

Is this the job that I am here to do? To help explain the nature of our world, where thoughts matter, and science and spirituality can be one. Perhaps it is. All I do know is that it brings me joy.

I think that is the key. To find what brings us joy and makes our spirit sing, whatever that may be. It is then that the spirit within can soar.

'Don't die with your music still inside you' is one of my favourite quotes from Wayne Dyer (American philosopher, self-help author and motivational speaker 1940 – 2015).

We all have our own music inside us – something we love or yearn to do, our passion, our gift, our purpose. The music inside you is your spirit within and your gift to yourself and to the world.

Let your spirit sing!

The Language Of The Spirit – How Music Heals Us

Andrea Sherko

Music is the language of the spirit.
It opens the secret of life, bringing peace, abolishing strife.

Kahlil Gibran

The Spirit Within

What is 'spirit'? It means different things to different people, both individually and collectively. For me, it is the intangible essence, beyond mind and body, that makes us complete. Without it, we remain two-dimensional, lacking substance and depth.

For many years, I had made a conscious decision to completely ignore this part of myself. I was dismissive of all forms of spirituality and religion and was convinced that there was nothing beyond the tangible: the things that I could see, hear, or touch. I had neglected my spirit for so long that it had wilted and withered almost to the point of extinction.

Around fifteen years ago, when I was in my early forties, I suddenly became unwell. I had been busy with work and study, and was starting to feel that I was finally making 'progress', in the material sense that is so highly valued in our society. Then, suddenly, I could hardly get out of bed in the morning. I was in pain all over and exhausted beyond belief. I had no idea what was happening to me.

After three years of doctors, drugs, and depression, I was finally diagnosed with Fibromyalgia. The diagnosis did not really help, as there is no 'cure' for this type of ailment. While medication helped to stabilise the condition, I knew that I needed more. My body was clearly sending me a message that I could no longer ignore.

Instinctively, I turned to music for help. Music had been an important part of my early life. As a young child, my mother sang to me, and taught me to read music and play the recorder. The record player in my home was rarely silent, emitting an eclectic mix of classical, folk, and popular music. Through primary and secondary school, I had lessons in a variety of instruments, and played in every available school ensemble. After leaving school, I studied music and attempted to become a professional musician. These attempts were unsuccessful, and I abandoned music, feeling disillusioned and defeated. I resolved to have nothing further to do with music again.

By the time I became ill, and like my spiritual self, I had neglected my musical self for years. What has become clear to me recently is that these two things – spirit and music – are for me, inextricably bound together. Spirit needs music to communicate, and music needs spirit for its powers of healing and connectivity.

In healing myself in mind, body, and spirit, I have found listening to music to be enormously beneficial. This is most often achieved when I follow a three-stage process of relaxation, reflection, and rejuvenation, as outlined below.

Relaxation

Given that stress is a major contributing factor to the symptoms associated with Fibromyalgia, it is important to address this issue at the beginning of each listening session.

I have found that various forms of chant (such as Gregorian or Buddhist) are particularly effective in helping me to relax my mind and body. By listening to the flow of the music and following its rising and falling, I begin to feel the tension leaving my body almost immediately. My shoulders relax, my fists unclench, and I become more aware of being 'in' my body.

The repetitive nature of chant helps to slow both my breathing and heartbeat. After five to ten minutes of this type of listening experience, I am feeling both mentally and physically relaxed and calm.

Reflection

Once I am relaxed, I can then be fully present in the moment and reflect. When I listen to music with my full attention, I am unable to dwell on past regrets or worry about future events; I can only reflect on feelings and emotions that I am currently experiencing.

The type of music I listen to at this stage of the process varies, but it tends to be instrumental rather than vocal; words would be a distraction, while instrumental music enables me to remain focused on my reflections.

It was during one of these periods of reflection that I first became aware that there is, indeed, 'something' beyond my own bodily experience. I felt as if I had transcended my tangible body – I could no longer see or hear anything – not even my intangible mind. I had made a connection at the level of pure consciousness: I felt that I had connected with something beyond time and place – I had connected with 'Spirit'.

Unlike many people, I do not believe that spirit is *super*natural; it is not an entity that can be characterised as 'he' or 'she'. Spirit seems to me to be a naturally occurring phenomenon, rather like gravity: we know that gravity exists because we see the consequences of its activity, even if we cannot actually see *it*. Regrettably, I know nothing at all about physics, but I like to think of spirit as positive energy, which manifests itself in and connects all living creatures.

Rejuvenation

Once my mind and body are relaxed, and my reflections have refreshed and reconnected my spirit to *the* spirit, the final stage of my musical self-healing involves increasing my physical energy levels to match the mental stimulation achieved in the previous stage.

The music I choose for this final stage tends to be fast, loud, and in cheerful major keys. I often listen to 'pop' music when I am feeling that I need a boost in physical energy: *Love Shack* by the B52s and *Waterloo* by ABBA are two examples that readily come to mind.

Waterloo, for example, is full of energy from the first electric chord. It is loud, upbeat, and makes me want to jump up and dance (and I *very* rarely dance). This song has additional impact due to its strong associations with my high school years, when I was young and healthy. Although this was not generally a good time in my life, music was always a safe and happy place of refuge for me, and this song reminds me of those positive feelings during an otherwise dark time.

By the end of these listening sessions, I feel enhanced well-being in my mind, body, and spirit. As an individual being, music helps me to be the best possible version of myself, given the constraints imposed by my medical condition. I feel better these days than I ever thought possible when I first became ill, and I have no doubt that I am also a better person, having (re)discovered the spiritual aspect of myself. I have progressed from merely existing as a two-dimensional being, to living fully in all three human dimensions.

From 'I' to 'We'

The power of spirit, communicating through music, however, extends far beyond such individual transformation: it brings people together as 'community', and can effect similar transformative change on the community as an identifiable entity in its own right.

The modern concept of 'community' is not always easy to grasp. It can, however, be identified by reference to (at least) three main characteristics: community may be of *place*, where people live in a particular geographical area; *identity*, where belonging is based on shared beliefs or interests (such as a church congregation or volunteers working at a charitable organisation); and/or *practice*, where people share activities and projects (such as a sporting club or community garden). It is also possible that a single community could fall into more than one of these categories.

It follows from this broad definition that I belong to more than one community: I *live* in Melbourne, Victoria, and Australia (three identifiable communities), and my *identity* is very closely aligned to the *practices* performed at my church (one community that belongs to two categories of community). While any of these communities could be considered from a musical perspective, I will focus on my church, as it is the musical community with which I am most involved.

Late in 2009, even though I was feeling better within myself, I was in serious danger of becoming socially isolated, as I had become too accustomed to staying at home due to my illness. I had lost contact with the work and study communities that I had previously belonged to and felt that I needed to make an effort to find a new 'tribe' to which I could belong. Once again, I turned to music for help.

It had been far too long for me to attempt to play any of the orchestral instruments that I had found so easy when I was young, so I decided to join a choir. My interest in traditional, choral music led me to the Anglican church in Brunswick, which had a very active musical life. When I joined this choir, I thought I was merely re-engaging with music; my involvement in the choir (and church), however, provided me with far more than just a musical opportunity.

At Brunswick, I discovered the joy of singing in community. Congregational singing of hymns and psalms is an important part of Anglican liturgy and enables the community to share and express its feelings and emotions, its joys and sorrows. I believe that we all need this balance of highs and lows; if music is always joyful or always mournful, we do not experience the full gamut of human emotions.

By joining the choir at Brunswick, I also became part of the wider church community. I became involved in the church's Opportunity Shop and Parish Council, which enabled me to feel a sense of belonging to multiple communities and acquainted me with a broad range of people. All of these connections and activities greatly enriched my life for five years, but none of this would have happened if not for the initial 'call' of music.

The communal power of music is not, of course, confined by religious boundaries. The recent proliferation of community choirs shows that people are discovering the many benefits that can be obtained through group music-making. Singing, in particular, is beneficial for physical and mental health, and leads to improved social and friendship networks and increased participation in other community activities, as I discovered first-hand at Brunswick.

This forging of musical community (whether sacred or secular) is, I believe, an example of spirit performing its most important work, that of bringing people together. Our society is largely focused on individual gratification and personal advantage, and it is often only in times of crisis that we see people 'band' together for the common good. It is this coming together for the common good that spirit facilitates, and it is through music that it communicates its important message of solidarity to us as the community of humanity.

Final Thoughts

Through music, spirit has 'saved' me from a life of metaphorical impoverishment. Individually, my physical and mental well-being is continually optimised through the music I listen to. In addition, spirit through music has enabled me to rediscover and nurture my previously neglected spiritual self, so that I am completed as an individual human being.

Even more importantly, spirit through music has re-connected me with community. As Aristotle once said, '[Hu]man is a social animal'. No human life is complete if lived solely in isolation. We need to connect and interact with other people to lead a satisfying, complete life.

The importance and potential of spirit through music to bring people together cannot be overstated. Just imagine if the governments of the world harnessed and used music as the valuable natural resource that it so obviously is. The possibilities really would be endless.

Keep Going

Rosalie Carr

Even when things get tough, never give up. There is a light at the end of the tunnel, and things do get better.

Rosalie Carr

I grew up in a typical Australian household in the 1960s. Dad worked all the time, and my mother was a housewife, always cleaning, washing, and cooking, unlike her daughter! We lived in a cul de sac in Pascoe Vale in one of the best neighbourhoods in the area. The neighbourhood children played in the street, going inside only when the streetlights came on or when dinner was on the table, which was usually 5.30 pm.

My two brothers are a lot older than me, having married and left home in their 20s. Luckily, I had the neighbourhood children for company. I was very close to my mother; she meant everything to me. If she was not in my sight, I experienced terrible separation anxiety. This went on for many years.

School never interested me; I was bullied and teased a lot for being shy, for having curly hair, for having an 'old' father, and the list goes on. I threw up every morning before school due to anxiety. I was terrified of the other kids and the teachers. Luckily, I befriended a girl at school who was similar to me in personality, and we became close. But sure enough, we were bullied and teased and called lesbians due to our close friendship. I was desperate to get away from that dreadful place called 'school'. I feigned sickness a lot, so eventually, Mum and Dad said I could leave school at 15 if I promised to go to business college. I would have promised to walk on broken glass if it meant I could leave school.

At 15, I did leave and was out of there with absolutely zero regrets. The girl that I was friends with had previously left school to attend another high school. I didn't consider that I might never see her again. Over the years, I often wondered what had happened to her and where she was.

Eight years ago, I found her on Facebook, and we met up for a coffee. It was like no years had passed, even though it had been 40 years since we had seen each other. We are, to this day, still friends, and I am so grateful for her friendship.

About the time I left school, I learned that I had three half-siblings, two brothers and one sister, all of whom were very much older than me. My father had been married and divorced previously. His ex-wife took the children from him, and he never saw them again. Dad did try to contact his daughter, but she didn't want anything to do with him. At 15 years of age, I did not understand the impact that would have had on my poor father. I recently found out that my half-sister died, aged 81. I never met her and feel disappointed about what could have been. I had always wanted a sister, but in those days, it was all 'hush hush', and the opportunity was missed.

At that time, however, I didn't worry about this. Business college was lots of fun. No bullying or teasing, no name-calling, what a relief! I was still incredibly shy and timid but managed to attend college and eventually found a job in the city working as a junior legal secretary. I loved that job, and I saved my money and went on a cruise around the Fijian Islands when I was 17. I had an absolute ball.

I returned from the cruise with terrible flu, so I had to take time off work. I received a phone call (landline, of course) from my boss at work telling me not to come back. I was fired for no real reason. Being the shy, timid girl that I was, I just accepted that and hung up the phone, crying uncontrollably. I told my father what had happened, and he immediately called my boss back and told him exactly what he thought of him. I was very upset but eventually found another job working in the office at the CBA Bank in Melbourne. That was in 1979, and I hated that job. They were great people, but the work was terribly boring. After two weeks working at the bank, I found another job working for solicitors in Melbourne.

Life went on; I loved the disco scene and spent most Friday and Saturday nights at the local disco.

The new job was good. I was pretty much doing the same administrative secretarial work I had done previously, but this time, I enjoyed it. On Thursday, the 18th of March 1980, my mother came to the city so we could have lunch together. We had our lunch and then went window shopping. Soon it was time for me to return to the office, so I kissed Mum goodbye and said, 'I'll see you at home later.' Little did I know that my life was about to change forever.

I worked on Elizabeth Street, so I had to cross from the corner of Lonsdale Street and Elizabeth Street to get to the office. Once the green light appeared to allow me to cross the road, I began walking and got to the middle of Elizabeth Street when I was run over by a car that had sped through a red light going from Elizabeth Street towards Flinders Street. The car collided with me, and I was thrown into the air, back onto the bonnet, and then hit the concrete with such force that my skull was split open, which subsequently caused my head injury. I was 18 years old.

I have no memory of this accident, which in many ways, changed my life. All of the information I have regarding what happened after I was injured was told to me. I was unconscious and in a coma for quite some time. I was told that as I lay on the concrete in Elizabeth Street after being hit by the car, somebody had called on a priest from a nearby church, and he rushed down to give me my last rites. They obviously thought I would die.

I was told about the circumstances of the accident by the police. I was left for dead on the corner of Elizabeth and Lonsdale Streets, but luckily the police were sitting in their car and saw the whole thing. The police chased the driver and finally caught him. I was rushed to Royal Melbourne Hospital in a very critical condition. The police informed my family and were told to come into the hospital to say goodbye. I was not expected to survive, but my determination and will to live, won through.

I didn't know how long I was in a coma, but I finally awoke to my parents by my bedside. My poor parents were distraught. Recovery took a long time, but I was determined to get my life back. Something within me wanted to fight and not give up. I was too young to die.

I had to stay in a rehabilitation hospital to relearn walking, talking, holding a pen, and holding a knife and fork; the simple things we all take for granted, but I had lost the ability to do these things due to my head injury. I had a broken bone in my left leg also; a small injury but very painful.

The rehabilitation hospital was a nightmare for me. I was alone and terrified. I just wanted to go home. My parents and family visited me often. I was allowed home on the weekends. I felt ashamed that this had happened to me and was desperate to be 'normal' again. I suffered from vertigo for a long time and was told that it would disappear over time. I still get vertigo, but not to the extent it was.

Each day my parents came in to visit me, I cried uncontrollably. I longed to be home in my own bedroom, near my loved ones. Eventually, my parents demanded I be discharged from the rehab hospital. Returning home was the best day of my life!

After two years of recovery, I returned to the workforce. I wasn't going to let my accident define me. My spirit was strong, and I wanted to move on with life.

In 1981 I married an Italian man, who I thought was the love of my life. How wrong I was. The marriage lasted four years, and I swore I would never marry again, and I never have. I was happy to be single again.

I found a job in 1984 working for solicitors. I loved it for a while. After some time, I decided to leave and found another job. You guessed it, working for solicitors. This job was fabulous, and I loved it. I befriended a girl who was a devout Christian and a beautiful person. We became very close. She decided to work in the Philippines, and she loved living there, but on returning to Melbourne, she was diagnosed with non-Hodgkin Lymphoma. In August 2011, at 48 years of age, my friend lost her battle. My best friend was gone.

I met a man in 1988 at a party, a month after my father passed away. We became close friends, and loved going to discos and dancing the night away. Life was fun, and after 18 months together, I became pregnant with our first son. He also had a son from a previous relationship. We moved in together, and life was busy, but we were happy, for a while.

He was from a typical Italian family. Family lunch every Sunday, usually began at 1 pm and finished around 7 pm. Pasta, cannolis, coffee; the food was delicious, and nobody ever went home hungry.

Over time we grew apart. Life wasn't fun anymore. Working full-time, with three children to take care of; life had its challenges. We were constantly exhausted. I was desperate to move house as the house we were living in was very small. With three growing children, I longed for a larger house.

We eventually moved to a larger house, but I never felt like it was home. I wanted more, but wasn't sure what I wanted.

I became a single parent of two boys and one girl in 1999. Over time things between my ex and I improved, and I now consider him one of my best friends. It's a classic case of, 'I can't live with him, but I can't live without him.'

Life has been difficult, and there have been many times I would have been happy to leave this world, but I soldiered on. I had to keep going. I've been hurt and disappointed by friends and relatives, but I now realise we are all human and nobody is perfect. That's not to say I want certain people in my life, I am quite content with letting those people go now. Until recently, I felt I had to 'fix' broken relationships and friendships, but now I realise not every person you meet is meant to be in your life forever. I still find some things hard to forgive, but I have learned that forgiveness is more for yourself, not for the other person/people.

My mother has been by my side throughout everything, and I am happy to call her my mother and my best friend. I visited my mother very often and loved spending time with her. She made me laugh.

Mum's behaviour began to change in and around 2003. My mother had a routine and was always up and out of bed by 8 am, had the bed made, and her bedroom blinds up. One day my brother called me and asked me to check on Mum. I went to her house at around 11 am, and she was still in her nightgown with the bed unmade, telling me there were noises coming from the heater.

I called someone to have a look at the heater, and he said there was nothing wrong with it. Mum also began to water her plastic plants. I just thought she was being silly and mucking around. The thought that she may have dementia never entered my mind. I think I was in denial. These unusual behaviours continued to occur, and eventually, my family and I had to face the fact that mum had the onset of Alzheimer's disease. Mum lived alone as my father died in 1988 from bowel cancer, so Mum was moved to an aged care facility. I began volunteering at her aged care facility just so I could be near her. Mum's condition deteriorated drastically, as did her memory. This once active, funny, switched-on woman was now a tiny, frightened old lady. It broke my heart to see Mum walking with a frame, not knowing who I was and not knowing where she was.

One morning in 2010, my friend and I were going to visit Mum, and as I was about to leave, my brother called me to say that Mum had passed away. Even though I expected this, it was still a shock. I didn't want to be without my mum in my life, but there was also a sense of relief that she was no longer suffering.

Mum's funeral was lovely, with a lot of people attending. Many of her nieces and nephews, who Mum hadn't seen for a long time, made the effort to attend her funeral. Before Mum's condition got too bad, she had told me that she wanted to die, and I understood her completely. Therefore, at her funeral, I did not cry. I think I was content with the knowledge that Mum was now at peace.

Mum's passing wasn't the only death that impacted me and my family. In December of 2008, I received a phone call from my eldest brother to say his son, had passed away due to suicide at 32 years old. I was lost for words. My nephew had lived with me for a while, and I could not see any signs that he wanted to die. In fact, he was a funny, hard-working young man, with many jokes to tell. I know that my nephew had an extremely difficult childhood due to an uncaring mother. His funeral was naturally very emotional. My brother and I viewed his body, and he looked so peaceful. The demons which had plagued him his entire life were no more.

Eleven years later, I got another call from my younger brother to say that my nephew, who lived in Queensland, had taken his own life. He was in his late 30's and had been diagnosed with bipolar disorder. His issues were many, and I guess this was his only way to find peace. I felt for my brother as this was his only son.

Suicide leaves us all with many questions and statements like, why would they do this? Was it my fault? I should have been there more. If only…. So I started writing my feelings down and turned a lot of my writing into poems. This has helped me immensely.

I miss my mother terribly, and in the early days of her passing, I began to drink to ease the pain. My drink of choice was red wine. I was a single mum of three kids, overwhelmed by everything in life, and drinking was all that helped. I managed to get the kids to school, came home and slept all day until it was time to pick up the kids from school. Not much changed for about ten years. Life was as normal as it could be. My time was spent driving kids to and from school and kids' activities. I sometimes would go a week without alcohol, which was an achievement for me. The funny thing about alcohol for me was that if I went without it for a long period, I'd reward myself with a drink. If I had a good day, I'd have a drink, and if I had a bad day, I'd have a drink

Alcohol ruled my life for a while, but I was becoming less tolerant of my becoming drunk and sought counselling. I have now overcome my problem with alcohol. I don't feel I need to reward myself any more, except maybe for the occasional chocolate.

In January 2017, my eldest son and his partner welcomed a baby girl into their lives. Becoming a grandmother for the first time was indescribable. I was there for her birth and fell in love with her immediately.

In October 2020, my daughter and her husband welcomed a baby boy into their lives. Once again, I fell in love. In November 2020, my son and his partner welcomed another baby girl into their lives. Again, I was at the birth, this time a home birth. Again, I fell in love with this child.

To me, my life was complete. I now had three beautiful grandchildren to love and help take care of.

In 2021, my eldest son, his partner and two daughters decided to live in New South Wales. My world fell apart, but I had to accept it. My other son decided to move out of home also. My daughter had married three years previously, so it had been myself and my son living together for a few years. He had been wonderful company, particularly during the lockdowns.

So, after 20-plus years of single motherhood, lots of chaos, lots of mess, lots of noise, I walked into my now empty, quiet house. I stood in the hallway wondering what I was going to do with my life and just cried. I stopped eating and lost weight (not complaining about that). One of the ways I coped was to write poetry. This is what I wrote:

The Price of Loneliness
To My Children

It was 2019.
What a horrible year.
Feeling loss and grief,
Plus feeling intense fear.
Not knowing how to be,
Not knowing what to do.

I did not know how life should be
Without all of you.
I slept a lot.
I thought a lot.
I wondered what was to be.
But most of all,
I wondered what was happening to me.
The price of loneliness led to wrong choices.
The price of loneliness led to hearing wrong voices.
I've made mistakes; I have done wrong.
If only those mistakes could all be undone.
You're all living your lives now,
And how proud can I be.
I am still suffering and miss you terribly
But I know in my heart,
That one day, I will be free.

I received mental health treatment at Broadmeadows Hospital, and they helped me so much. Joining Meetup groups has been great too. I've met many wonderful people, and my social life is very busy.

Life has often been difficult for me, but I am a stronger woman for it. I have recently been diagnosed with bipolar depression, but I will never give up and will keep going.

I love hearing other people's stories, and I continually strive to learn. I am now doing a basic hairdressing course simply because it is something I have always wanted to do. Finally, at 61 years old, I am enjoying life and look forward to completing the hairdressing course and seeing what life has in store for the future.

Oh The Places You'll Go!

Christine Carmuciano

'You're off to Great Places! Today is your day! Your mountain is waiting, so...get on your way!'

Dr Seuss

The Spirit Within

The spirit within?

What is the spirit within? What does that mean? What is your spirit?

Is it what gets you up every morning, your drive to conquer another day?

Is it what makes you fight to exist, or is it something more?

If I have to be honest, I've struggled quite a bit with this concept, 'The spirit within'.

What keeps me going? I know I have a drive within me; God knows I've had my fair share of hardships and have survived them all. So obviously, I do have a drive, a 'spirit' within me that keeps me moving ever forward. But what is it? Is it tangible, or is it innate, kind of like 'fight or flight'? As the saying goes, 'When the going gets tough, the tough get going!'

I know from a very young age, I've always thought there must be more out there. I've always wanted to look outside the box, not just accept the box I was born into. I've discussed, argued and pleaded my case countless times, especially with my dear old dad, that there is more to life than just getting up every morning, going to work, just to do it all again the next day and for the rest of our lives. Talk about groundhog day!

But the irony in that is, since I resigned from my long-term career with the bank and have the time on my hands that I have longed for, I am now lost. I find myself struggling to find what my identity is now. What is my purpose now?

Of late, I must admit that sometimes I feel that I have lost my spirit within. My drive to push on. I feel like I have lost my identity. I question who I am now. I have no 'real' job; I don't earn the income I used to, and I no longer have a 'status' or something I can say that I am.

So who am I?

Surely my career wasn't all I was?

What I have realised over the past eighteen months since leaving my full-time job, is that I based my worth and value on what my role was in life. I was always 'something'!

Obviously, I was a daughter and still am, of course. I was a relatively good student and one that eagerly wanted to assert my independence by starting part-time work at the legal age of fourteen years and nine months at our local supermarket. I then dutifully became a wife, and a mother, but unfortunately, by the time my children were in their primary school years, I became a single mother. And the list goes on; I was a hairdresser, a medical receptionist, a teller, a sales and service adviser, a personal banker and home loan specialist and later, a file quality analyst. Not to mention other incidental jobs thrown into the mix.

Then I was nobody. I was on a break. But who was I?

I was supposed to find this out during this time of hiatus, but all I found was that I didn't know who I was. I didn't have a 'status' anymore; I was a nobody. This is what I told myself, what I believed in my own mind. I had no value anymore. I didn't earn an income, so therefore, I had no value. Even though I was indebted to no one, as I lived alone and had for quite some time, I only had myself to depend on financially. So why did I feel like I was letting myself down?

I had an awakening when in a course I was participating in. I was asked to write an introduction about myself on their Facebook group page. The first thing I noticed when I read everyone else's introduction about themselves, was that everyone had some sort of title or a few next to their name, and all mine had was my old school that I went to back in 1979. Surely there was more to me than that?

Even Facebook didn't think so! (Mainly due to the fact that I hadn't added further information as I didn't think anything I had previously accomplished was worthy or notable.) But when I began to write my introduction and speak about my life from the time I finished with my previous employer, I had actually not stood still in all that time. I had completed a Cert III in

Education Support, I had written a chapter in a book that was now published, and I had travelled to Egypt, a dream since I was very young. Oh, and I also managed to complete an Art Therapy course and obtain a diploma, thanks to Covid 19 and not being able to go anywhere because we were in lockdown.

Yet still, I did not value myself!

I felt I wasn't worthy anymore as I didn't have a title against my name, even though I had accomplished all these things. Why was this not enough? What did I give value to?

It certainly wasn't myself! It seemed that no matter what I did, in my eyes, it was never enough. It was not good enough! I wasn't as good as others around me. I compared myself constantly, which only validated my story even more. I had done nothing during this time.

Why did I place value on what I did and not in who I was?

Where was my spirit within? Where had it gone?

De-valuing myself is something I do quite well. I have quite often felt that I am not good enough or as good as others. Why? I believe fear holds me back quite a bit. Fear of leaving any comfort zone can cripple me until I finally take the jump. Why does it take me so long?

Why can I not just jump without fear halting me in my tracks?

Because it's easier to make excuses that validate your own story, that you're not good enough, so that you don't have to come out of the shadows. It says, 'That's OK, you just stay there, you don't have to grow. You can stay exactly as you are and where you are, but then why are you complaining that you want more? If you want more, then you need to step out from behind those shadows and show yourself.'

Don't you just love that inner voice? That power within? The lightbulb moment! There it is! **My power within! My Spirit within!** It's that inner voice that keeps driving me, challenging me and pushing me not to give up. It's that drive that just won't let me settle. That need to know more and explore outside the parameters, outside what my parents cautioned me against (for my own safety, of course, or was it their own fear?)

Now I realise that is and always has been my power within, my spirit within. My inner voice! My higher self!

At times I watch the bus outside my window pass by routinely and observe my life in the same way. Every day turns into every month, which turns into every year and what seems suddenly, I am here in the age and body I am now.

Our life can seem just like the bus going by routinely on the same road, reliable and following its schedule. Is that what many of us do, follow the road we're supposed to be on? Who determines that road? Our parents, our environment, peer group pressure, fear of not fitting in with the 'norm'? I have found that it is only when we veer off that road, whether that be by accident or design, that our world opens up, and we discover new roads and new ways of being.

From a young age, I found that I was always questioning and searching. I really didn't know what for, but basically, I felt that my world was not enough. It felt very small. Surely there was more! I wanted to explore and travel the world. I dreamt of living overseas and experiencing different cultures. Maybe it was my Italian roots beckoning me, along with my mother's stories of her younger years, that I constantly felt this inexplicable longing.

One of my earliest memories of daydreaming my time away was of me as a young girl in primary school, sitting on the front fence of my family home in Fawkner. Daydreaming of what my life would be like and what adventures might come my way, as I watched the day-to-day life pass me by. Watching people coming and going, I could entertain myself for hours while my imagination ran wild, and I created and embedded myself in my own little world.

Although I wasn't an only child, sometimes I felt like I was. I was the youngest and only girl, with two older brothers, one ten years my senior and the other five. My memories growing up were, at times, of loneliness; though I had friends, I obviously couldn't be with them all the time. I remember many times complaining to my mother, 'Why did you never give me a sister?' (Like it was that easy!).

So although I grew up with brothers and supportive parents, I still had many times when I felt lonely. The irony is, that I still do. I can't seem to shake that feeling of loneliness, even as an adult.

I'm still to unpack that emotion and often wonder why it still impacts me today. I think I know where it stems from, though, obviously my childhood, right? Isn't that what we automatically think? But why do I still feel that way many times, even when I am with people? I often question whether I really do belong when I am in a group. Even if they are familiar to me, these questions often make me wonder if there is more to life as we know it. Could these feelings have transcended from another lifetime?

Have I carried this from past lives, and my purpose in this lifetime is to finally heal this part of my soul? Now I know some of you reading this might struggle with this concept, carrying wounds from past lives into this lifetime. Or maybe just the mention of past lives is freaking you out. I get it!

It wasn't until I started exploring spirituality that I considered this more and more. Not that I have the answer, and I am certainly not here to convince you either way, but maybe just consider the possibility. Religion can be traced back centuries with references to reincarnation. The Buddhists, for example, believe that the soul will continue to come back to this world until you learn from your lessons, right your wrongs and ultimately reach enlightenment. I can remember doing an assignment on this back in secondary school and how much it intrigued me then. Many of us believe we have a soul which is not bound to this body once its time on earth expires. So where does our soul go? I have my belief, but I won't bore you with that. I'll leave that for you to decide.

I do know that spirituality opened up so much for me, although I probably wouldn't have known to call it 'spirituality' back then. I suppose I called it God and still do in many ways. I'm learning that we have so many helpers who look out for us, and I am loving the journey of discovering this and trusting in them, our Angels, our Ancestors, Spirit Guides, God, and The Universe. At the end of the day, it is all a spiritual energy that, when tapped into, can open up so much in our life.

Trust is the key, and believe me, many times, that is very hard to do. To relinquish control and be patient, knowing that what we wish for will come to us only if and when it is right for us. I know from experience that this can be a difficult pill to swallow, and with it comes some hard, sometimes painful lessons. Yet it always finds a way to work out as it is meant to and place you exactly where you need to be.

Personally, I believe that our power within shines brightest every time we pick ourselves up after falling down. The ability to admit when you're wrong, face the consequences and still hold your head up in the process is the ultimate display of innate power. These are all inner strengths that we don't give enough credit to. Being able to constantly re-evaluate yourself and a situation, learn from your mistakes and grow from it, is a power within. It is the spirit within that keeps driving us, or me anyway.

Staying stagnant and forthright in my opinion of how something should or shouldn't be still holds me today; it does not allow me to move forward. In fact, I find that it actually diminishes my power within, as it is only my ego that is keeping me on that path of indignation, not my spiritual or higher self. It is in these situations when I am confronted with my shadow self, which can be a difficult reflection to look back at. Yet as hard as it is sometimes, it is these times that allow me to truly reflect, recognise and grow. It is only through our conflicts and challenges that we are called to dig deep and find that power within us so that we can become better versions of ourselves.

I came across something in my art therapy course, which I completed during the Covid lockdown, around body image, and it really resonated with me. I know that I constantly tell myself how 'fat' I am and 'look at that stomach; it's huge!' Even though I know better and am aware of how detrimental this actually is to me.

The chapter was on self-esteem and body image, and one of the activities was to write down what you thought about yourself and then what you thought about someone you love. The list about myself contained much about my physical body and my negatives, yet the list for the person I loved had nothing to do with their physical body, only all their attributes and personality. I described how caring and loving they are and everything I love about them, nothing to do with their body. So why is it that we cannot see the positives in ourselves? Why do we treat ourselves so harshly when we would never do that to someone that we love? 'Love' being the operative word.

This is the lesson we, or I, need to learn; to love ourselves and our whole body, the good bits and the not-so-great bits. Look at it with gratitude for more than just its exterior, and thank it, for without it sustaining us as it does, we would not be here or living the life we are. I can personally attest to this! My body has some obvious scars, but they are all a reminder that I am still alive, so how can I not be grateful for them?

Note to self, be kind to yourself and learn to love who you are, not just see yourself as the physical self. It's a work in progress! Especially now, as I find myself as a, well as society says, 'a middle-aged woman'. This does not sit well with me, as I don't feel like I am a middle-aged woman. How can I be when I'm still that young girl inside, who still has so many dreams she'd like to fulfil? Maybe she is the one that drives me and is my spirit within?

I am living in a generation where there are so many women (and men) out there my age who find themselves alone, many due to divorce. It seems to be its own pandemic; people searching for bigger and better, younger and prettier, that elusive grass that is supposed to be so much greener on the other side. Is it? Maybe for some, but maybe for many, it isn't so green after all.

To be honest, many times, I find myself a little scared and worried about my life. What will it be like as I get older? The children have well and truly left the coop and have their own families. So who do I sit and chat with at night or go to when I have a problem or just need some sort of reassurance or that feeling of security? Someone to just put their arm around me and say, 'It'll be ok'. I must admit these thoughts do occupy my mind sometimes, generally as soon as my head hits the pillow. Who needs sleep anyway? It can feel quite overwhelming when you allow yourself to dwell on your aloneness and what life will look like as you get older.

Never before had I really thought about getting old and my own mortality, but more and more now, I find that it hovers around in the crevices of my mind, just enough to know it's there. Hopefully, it remains dormant for a long time to come. It does, however, conjure up memories of my mother and her decline, more so in the last three years of her life, which were mainly spent in a nursing home.

That was a big wake-up call, walking through the main area to visit her, seeing all those people who were once like you and me and now spend most of their days in a chair, waiting for someone to visit or spend some time with them. Others are not even aware of their surroundings. All of these people with their own stories and a time in their life when they were young and vibrant too.

My mother was also one of these people in the end, an intelligent and beautiful woman, a trailblazer who was determined and independent for her time. In the end though, her body let her down, and all she could do was lay in bed, looking up to the ceiling. Or was she looking past that, somewhere much higher where time had no meaning? Was she being called, preparing herself in her silent voice? Could she hear her ancestors, mother and father, her siblings gone before her? Were they calling her and telling her that her time was approaching, but not just yet? 'Be patient, my daughter. Your time is near.'

I truly believe she hung on for my brother; his untimely death sent the family into a downward spiral, the shock too great for all. She knew then it was her time, as she passed only two days after him. Was there something far greater, beyond what our human brains can comprehend, that kept her here until she knew it was the exact time for her to leave?

I would sometimes stand outside her room, watching her. Laying there with her arm raised up to the heavens. What could she see? Who was she seeing?

I like to think it was all her loved ones gone before her and an army of angels preparing her way. It was so bright; a warmth could be felt throughout her body. It was freedom! She would finally be released from the prison that was her body.

Her final breath - it felt like in an instant her soul took off like a rocket, and she was gone. I looked at my daughter, and we couldn't believe our eyes. Or was it an inner knowing that we both just felt? It felt so tangible! She was gone and finally free. Her body now an empty vessel. I felt sad but, at the same time, relief for her. She was now free, being greeted by all her loved ones who had been preparing her homecoming. She could now be there for her son, who needed her more than the ones she had left behind. I couldn't help but feel so much love and grief at the same time.

I believe the spirit within never leaves us; it is beyond this realm. Just like the umbilical cord that binds us with our children from their conception and development, and even though this cord is cut at birth, I believe it is only the physical cord that is cut and that we are bound together for all eternity. Just like my mother made the decision to leave when she did, it transcended all time and physicality. She was still there, her spirit shining bright and performing its most selfless act right until the end of her physical life. She was going to be there for her son when he needed her the most, knowing that all her loved ones still on this earthly plane would be okay and would take care of each other until we all meet again.

I don't know about you, but for me, it makes it all the easier to bear because I know we will meet again. I feel my mother's energy around me always, and I have no doubt that she is present in everything my family and I do. I'm sure she guides us in her subtle ways, just as she did when she was here. Although sometimes, maybe not so subtle.

So, therefore, is the spirit within; LOVE?

Unconditional and overwhelming love can power through anything and resurrect the darkest day. A simple hug can break down all barriers and make you feel loved, protected and that you are not alone in this world. LOVE transcends all realms, past, present and future. That loving energy can be felt anywhere. It transcends time and space.

So is it as simple as that? Is the spirit within, unconditional love? Unconditional love for others and unconditional love for ourselves?

I recently listened to an interview by a woman named Samantha Nolan-Smith, from the School of Visibility, where she spoke about points in our life where we lose our confidence. Her talk was mainly centred around women. The first point is when you transition from a child to a teenager, free of any inhibitions, to suddenly becoming aware of your body and then comparing yourself to others. Society tells you that you need to look a certain way to be beautiful, and therefore you must not be beautiful if you do not fit this unrealistic stereotype.

This is possibly our first major experience of losing our confidence and questioning our own value, although with social media, sadly, I believe this happens even younger these days.

The second point is when you become a mother. You leave your place in society where you had a voice and a 'value' to ultimately put your life on hold so that you can rear the next generation. (Disclaimer, this can also relate to a man, but I am speaking from a more personal experience and, in this case, more about women.) This transition can definitely cause many women to lose their confidence. We go from talking to leaders and colleagues to becoming a linguist, proficient in baby talk. At times this can have an adverse effect on a young mum, especially in the early months when most of her days revolve around four walls and her baby.

The third point in your life where you lose your confidence is where I see myself at now, where you transition into an 'elder'. Someone who has lived life and had experiences but is now invisible. Where other societies revere and respect their elderly, our society quite often looks upon this generation as 'not knowing what they're talking about'. Being elderly is seen as a weakness rather than a strength, and elders are often ignored despite their ability to offer sage advice from their life and experiences.

What I loved about this talk is that Nolan-Smith normalised the feeling of 'losing your confidence'. That question of 'who am I now?' was being validated. I was not alone in feeling that at times I felt like I was no longer heard or had a voice.

Interestingly enough, my daughter not so long ago, had a heart-to-heart with me and, in no uncertain terms, told me it was time to, 'Get my power back!' Why was I acting like a scared little bird at times when I was around them? Too scared to 'step on anyone's toes'. 'Where did the mother, who was so strong, independent and determined, go? What has happened to her?'

Coming from a place of love and concern for me, but with conviction, she informed me that 'enough was enough' and it was time to 'get my act together' and once again be that strong woman, not someone who has given up and cowers to people, afraid to speak up.

Was that who I was becoming? Had I lost my confidence? Why?

I had always prided myself on how 'strong' a woman I was, so why was I becoming a lesser version of myself?

Maybe it was normal for me to feel this because that's exactly the point in my life where I am. The point in my life where I have to find my place again, where I don't have to fight for or protect anyone anymore. Where I need to re-define what the spirit within me is? Discover what is going to drive me now.

For a time, on becoming a grandmother, I thought my role was now to help my children and to carry out the grandmotherly duty of being available whenever they needed babysitting or anything else they required. But more and more I found that my children didn't need me; other than my availability, they didn't actually need ME anymore. So who was I? Maybe it wasn't enough, like I had been telling myself, to just be there for my family. Maybe the spirit within had to become selfish and explore who I was now, minus the wife title, the daughter title, the mother title and now the grandmother title.

Maybe instead of avoiding putting myself first and thinking my duty was to everyone else first, it was time to be selfish. I needed to 'allow' everyone to live their own journey, the highs and the lows. It was for them to experience, and I had to accept it was no longer my job to protect them. Because ultimately, what am I protecting them against? My own fears? As my daughter said to me, I should be proud that they don't need me anymore. I have done my job. It was time to let go. I just have to discover what my 'label' is now.

Maybe, true to one of my own essential oil blends that I have created, I need to find that 'Bohemian' woman inside of me. That spirit within that is freedom, self-love, forgiveness and evolution. Not worrying about what others think or what my programming has indoctrinated in me for so long. Surely it is time to finally allow myself to put ME first and not feel bad about it!

So in a long winded kind of way, I believe the spirit within can mean so many things. Your Higher Self, Your inner knowing, Unconditional Love and that everlasting Soul energy that lives on regardless of time or space. Ultimately for me, I know that when I am most true to myself and come from a place of love and gratitude, not only for myself but for others too, I am most in tune with my spirit within. I hear the messages it conveys to me through my intuition and the subtle signs it sends to my gut when something feels right or wrong. When I am closest to feeling love and giving love and am able to block out the white noise, I am able to hear and can be more at one with my spirit within.

It is that which constantly challenges me to search for my true purpose and not become complacent, all the while honouring my true self and not dismissing, patronising or berating myself in the process. And above all, reminding myself that my spirit within will always be its brightest and most powerful when I love myself and my decisions without regret; when I trust my spirit to guide me and when I fill my cup until it overflows.

So although I find myself in a state of limbo, not knowing which peg I fit into; I know that my story is only partially written and that there is still so much out there for me. It's just not tangible yet. What I do know though, is that I can feel it with all my being! So until my soul feels nourished again and my heart is full, maybe it is time to let go and follow the spirit within me wherever it wants to go!

Just like the book my son once gifted me, Dr Seuss,' *Oh, The Places You'll Go*!. And the beautiful reminder he wrote to me on the inside cover, a quote originally written by Robert Schuller; 'Tough times don't last, but tough people do!'

The journey will surely take you over hill and dale, and you'll certainly come across some roadblocks along the way, but there'll also be many amazing moments along the way too. And it is all of these things that will make up the story of your life and allow you to discover and rediscover the spirit that is within you.

So in this next chapter in my life, I vow to listen more to the spirit within me, the inner child I have suppressed for so long and embrace this middle-aged woman that is now me and follow Dr Seuss wherever he wants to take me.

Hell, maybe I'll even let my hair go grey! Or maybe not!

Life In Pieces Through Dreams

Dawn Sulley

Negative thoughts never give you a happy life. Be amazing today! Never give up anything is possible.

Dawn Sulley

The Spirit Within

As a child, when the sun went down each evening, I would start to feel anxious, and would have a sense of fear before falling asleep.

I would fall asleep seeing myself standing on the tarmac of an airfield, with a very old plane slowly coming towards me. The plane would stop just short of me, and I would be looking upwards and see a propeller spinning at my eye level. Then I drifted off to sleep. This would happen almost every evening.

Once I fell asleep, my dreams would begin with blue snakes all around me. I would be standing on top of the kitchen table, feeling trapped. This then merged into me watching a young boy standing on a train, dressed in shorts and a white shirt, with blonde curly hair. He was happy and smiling.

The train would come to a stop outside the house where I was living with my foster family. The boy would get off the train, knock on the backdoor and call my name. I would wake up and try to make sense of these dreams.

It wasn't until I was nineteen that I started to gain an understanding of the significance of these dreams. My sister and I met our biological grandmother (Nana). During our emotional conversations about our family upbringing, we were told of our strong Irish, English and European connections. I finally understood why I seemed to gravitate towards people from foreign cultures.

Nana showed my sister and me around her home in South Gippsland. Whilst showing us her bedroom, I was drawn to a framed photograph of a young boy on the wall. I asked Nana, 'Who is that boy?' Nana explained that he was Trevor, my half-brother. He died after falling from a train en route to Bendigo.

Nana explained that she had tried to stop him from falling out of the open carriage doors. She had called out, 'The bene! The bene!' but no one could understand what she was saying because of her strong English accent. She was trying to say the baby was about to fall out the open doors of the train and was desperate for anyone to help.

Trevor fell. The driver stopped the train, and the passengers were told to stay on the train, whilst the driver went back to look for him. Trevor was on the track, lifeless. An ambulance was called along with the police. Trevor was taken to the Bendigo hospital, where he was pronounced deceased. Nana blamed herself. When recounting this story, her eyes welled up. Nana still struggled with what had happened thirty years prior!

I recognised Trevor as the boy from my childhood dreams. Nan was astonished when I relayed my dreams to her. I had finally connected the dreams to my family, the missing piece! Validation!

We were all crying, and I had goosebumps.

It took a long time for me to process this. My sister understood, as I had discussed this with her many times. At the time, she thought I was crazy, but she quickly changed her mind after hearing Nana's story about our brother Trevor.

I have always felt a spiritual connection.

My spiritual beliefs are more than just religious, although I believe in a 'God' of some kind, and I have explored various Christian religions.

There are many definitions of spirituality. Any of them can help us understand this important yet mysterious part of life. Ultimately, none of them captures the whole reality. I believe that your inner energy is part of your spirituality, your soul. This is expressed in every aspect of your personal and public life. It is part of the person you are, and every person has some form of spirituality. Whatever moves or expresses your spirit or inner energy is part of your spirituality. In my view, our spirituality is just part of who we are, woven into and expressed through our every thought, feeling, and action.

I dealt with issues such as identity, loss of purpose and unexplained feelings of not belonging. What makes such matters spiritual is that they raise questions about the meaning of life, life in general and my life in particular. I realised I have always been a spiritual person when I began analysing the nightly dreams I had as a child.

I express my spirituality through believing in higher powers and life forces. I use this spiritual energy to nurture relationships with family, friends and the wider community. It empowers me to give and receive love, support, kindness, guidance, loyalty and, most importantly, forgiveness.

I try to express myself creatively through art, by listening to music, writing, appreciating visual and performing arts attending concerts, watching movies, and reading. I enjoy engaging in conversations with friends and family about the meaning of life. I pay attention to the movements in my emotional life when I feel the spirit within myself. I look for hope, compassion, love, trust, and forgiveness. These are important in my search for meaning within relationships. I feel I grow spiritually as I learn to nurture these things.

Spiritual experiences

My trip to Ireland in 2016 also brought me closer to the spirit within me. As soon as we landed, I immediately felt at home. As my husband and I started our nine-day tour. I was very excited to be there. My ancestors originated from the county of Cork and Munster. They emigrated to Australia in the 1800s during the potato famine. Strangely, our tour of Ireland included an invitation to a four-course banquet at Bunratty Castle. Here we enjoyed the Bunratty singers and dancers in the Great Hall of the castle. On arrival, the guests were permitted to walk around the park grounds. Two young girls dressed as maidens came up to my husband and me with an invitation for us to play the parts of the king and queen of Munster. What a fabulous evening it turned out to be!

I experienced many sensations of 'deja vu' in Ireland. There were many places that we visited, where I felt that I had been before. This was especially true when we were cruising on the River Shannon. A band was playing beautiful Irish music, and I started crying uncontrollably. I felt overwhelming sensations of happiness and sadness, almost simultaneously.

But my spirituality was perhaps needed the most when I was diagnosed with cancer.

Being diagnosed with stage four Ovarian Cancer created a fear within me I had never felt before. The unknown was happening. This was a terrifying new part of my 'life experiences'. On the positive side, I had a chance to open myself to the resources and depths of my spiritual side. This validated the support I already receive with the love of my husband, family, friends and others.

Thinking this way has helped me fill my life with hope, purpose and inner peace.

When I was first diagnosed, I felt a great sense of denial. The first line of treatment involved seven hours of surgery called debulking, which meant removing as much of the cancer as safely as possible. (I was told the surgical team managed to get 95% of the cancer.)

Life in Pieces Through Dreams

This was followed by chemotherapy to knock out the rest of my cancer.

After surgery, I was transferred to the critical care unit. Whilst in the unit, I felt my death was near. I felt as though I was in a cloud, half in this world and half in an unknown, very surreal place. For about three days, I could hear voices and humming. I could see my deceased elder brother Ian; he was wearing a blue shirt and had curly blonde hair. His arms were crossed, and he was leaning against a tree watching a circle of native Americans in full dress colour, with feathers and long plaited dark hair. They were sitting in a circle, humming around a smoking fire.

During this time, I could see an uncle of mine who had passed away three weeks prior to my cancer diagnosis. I could hear him talking to my foster mum, Phyllis, his sister. He was in his work clothes leaning over a suburban backyard fence. He was pulling some branches away to have a better look. He appeared to be looking down a driveway, and he kept repeating, 'No, she's not here, Phil. I can't see her. She's not coming.'

I had found my mindset changing. I decided I wanted to live, as I felt there was more for me to accomplish.

Having a healthy spiritual belief gives me a sense of peace and balance among the physical, emotional, and social aspects of my life. Being in nature or anywhere outside where there is fresh air will always bring benefits to a person's well-being. Spending time in nature, even if that means a walk around your local park, is an effective component of self-care.

The beach is my 'must-stop' for a full mind-body reset. Walking on the soft sand with occasional dips in the ocean with rolling waves landing on the beach, watching the sunset. This always serves as my happy place. Personal stresses, medical appointments, essentially all my real-world issues simply just melt away.

Two quotes in particular, helped me focus on my spiritual wellness. I hope they help you too.

Happiness is the spiritual experience of living every minute with love, grace, and gratitude. (Denis Waitley)

Being happy doesn't mean that everything is perfect. It means that you've decided to look beyond the imperfections. (Gerard Way)

The Path(s) To Enlightenment

Stephen D'Agata

We are not part of a multi-verse. Therefore, we must all have a singular origin and a shared creation story. Does that mean that there must be a definitive creator? Does it matter that different cultures have different beliefs about how we came to be? Intuitively, many of us know that there is more to life than mere biological existence. That we acknowledge and celebrate this spiritual awareness in many and varied ways reflects our cultural diversity and is essentially, just different means of achieving the same end.

Stephen D'Agata

In the messages at the end of my previous contribution to this anthology series, *A Message to your Younger Self*, I stated that: 'There is a God, but she is not what you think.' The key words here are: 'a God'. That is, a singular entity, and my use of the feminine pronoun should lead you to conclude that I am not referring to an old white man with a grey beard and flowing robes.

Despite being born and raised in the Roman Catholic faith and having been somewhat active in the Church as an adult, I always had progressive views. So, I was never of the opinion that there is one true faith. Unquestioning is not how you would describe my belief system.

I believe that we are spiritual beings temporarily housed in a biological skin. We share the one planet within a known universe that contains trillions of stars and planets. Astrophysics tells us that this universe was formed during a singular cataclysmic event referred to as the big bang. To my mind, it is ludicrous to believe that the spirit within us can have a variety of sources. So, whatever our spiritual belief system, we all must share the same origin and the same destiny.

Over the past two million years of human existence, each and every culture and society has developed its own origin stories as a means of reconciling our intuitive spirituality with our physical existence. These origin stories are remarkably similar, and they all emphasise that we have a spiritual connection with the universe and each other.

However, as social animals, we also share a need to belong to a tribe or a pack. Our individual origin stories thus evolved into rituals and belief systems that would define our cultural make-up. Cultural leaders would take advantage of this, and use this inherent need to belong, as a means of control. This eventually led to the formation of what we know now as organised mainstream religions.

The mainstream religion to which I belong is Roman Catholicism. It is the faith I was born into and was the faith of my ancestors for many centuries. It shares its Abrahamic origins with Judaism and Islam, which can be traced back many millennia. Like many others of Southern European and West Asian descent, my religious affiliation is part of my cultural make-up.

For most people who choose to identify as Catholic, this cultural connection is enough. They see themselves as good decent people who care for their fellow man, and sacraments, such as Baptism, First Communion, Confirmation, and Holy Matrimony, are largely seen as cultural rites of passage. Providing that they go through the motions, occasionally attend services, and defer to the clergy for spiritual guidance, they are fulfilling their religious obligations, and the church hierarchy is happy to keep them as members of the Catholic club.

My problem is that, as a teenager, I decided to investigate the religion more closely, and for my generation, this all happened at a time shortly after the 2nd Vatican Council, when the Catholic Church was going through a reformation of sorts. So, the religion I got to know was more closely aligned to the concept of a universal church, as opposed to a doctrinal church. Little was I to know that this was a short-lived hiatus, and the church hierarchy would soon regroup to reimpose doctrinal controls.

***

Growing up as a Roman Catholic in suburban Melbourne in the 1960s and 1970s, I received my primary education in the local Parish school. There we learned about the 10 commandments, the angels and saints, and heaven and hell. We deferred all authority on all things spiritual to the priests and other religious people. Our religious texts would depict God as rays of sunlight streaming through clouds. Saints and holy people were always drawn with halos. At Sunday Mass I could actually see halos around the heads of our priests. So, I knew that they must be holy persons. These halos would however disappear when, at the age of 13, I was diagnosed as being short-sighted and got my first pair of glasses.

Being one of seven siblings, my parents could not afford the additional fees associated with sending us all to Catholic secondary schools. My eldest brother got that opportunity and had to take the train to school every day wearing his red blazer and red cap. But the rest of us made do with walking to the local government high school. Once at high school, I discovered that not all Christians were Catholic. Everyone was, of course, Christian. Mosques and Temples would not feature in the community for at least another 20 years. But, although everyone seemed to have a religious affiliation, hardly anyone went to services on a Sunday. It was just not a huge part of their lives. In this environment, I was in a position where I could question my own belief systems and decide whether it was necessary for me to maintain my Sunday obligations.

Primary school had provided me with a good grounding in religious doctrine but had not provided me with any real spiritual enlightenment. But rather than giving up on the Church altogether, I decided to investigate further.

Attendance at a weekend youth retreat led to an invitation to consider becoming a Catechist, which is essentially a Sunday School teacher. Becoming a Catechist would involve training and attendance at religious retreats with adults. This is how, at the tender age of 14, I started receiving an advanced theological education. Meanwhile, my peers who stayed within the Catholic school system continued to be taught religion as a subject and would not experience anywhere near the spiritual enlightenment that I was benefitting from.

With all this happening shortly after the 2nd Vatican Council, the priests and other religious people leading my spiritual development at that time, were also looking beyond the doctrinal church and promoting a more empirical view of religion. I learned that the Church was first and foremost, the community of the faithful and not about buildings, icons, rituals, and hierarchy. This belief system, which was taught to me within the confines of Roman Catholicism, is consistent with my current understanding that we are all spiritual beings within a biological skin. That is why I have no problem in identifying as a Roman Catholic even though the Roman Catholic Church may have problems identifying with me.

***

Through most of my adult life, I continued to be actively involved in the Catholic Church. I served on Pastoral Councils at three separate parishes and continued to enjoy the company and guidance of the same sort of enlightened, progressive individuals who had influenced my religious development as a teenager. However, I was soon to discover that there were those within the church hierarchy for whom this enlightenment and progressiveness was a serious concern. Providing congregations with the skills to think for themselves about theological matters, was moving people away from the Church. They saw that the only way to redress this exodus was to return to traditional, pre-Vatican II, values.

It began subtly in the early noughties. I was working in a regional town and my wife Maria, and I were building our young family. The local parish priest was a remarkable person who saw that the only way for the

Church to survive was to provide the congregations with more responsibility and control. The failure of the Church to progress on the reforms initiated by the 2nd Vatican Council by permitting priests to marry and considering women clergy, led to a serious decline in priest numbers. In the city parishes, the days of parish priests working with one or two assistant priests were long gone, but, in regional parishes, the aging priest population were often called upon to administer to two or more parishes. Daily services were a thing of the past, and some smaller parishes were missing out on weekly Sunday services.

Our parish priest saw the writing on the wall and knew that, as he was close to retirement, it was unlikely that our Parish would get a new full-time priest once he was gone. His solution to this was to skill up the congregation so that they could run the parish on their own. This skills transfer would extend to holding Sunday services without a priest whenever necessary. Such services were known as Communion Services and were led by lay persons. They included all parts of the Mass apart from the Eucharistic Prayers (you need a priest to do the magic transubstantiation bit), and pre-consecrated hosts were issued for communion.

Apparently, although Communion Services were fine and dandy for weekdays, having one on a Sunday crossed a line with the Diocese. Our parish priest was advised that he must secure the services of a substitute priest if he was unavailable. Our priest replied to the bishop that suitable substitute priests were not readily available. Furthermore, most of the priests that he knew might be available were not the sort of priests that he wanted anywhere near his parishioners. Point taken, the bishop went out of his way to ensure that suitable priests were available to us when necessary, and Sunday communion services ceased to be a thing.

A few years later, work had taken me back to Melbourne, and I became a pastoral counsellor in another Melbourne parish. This parish employed the services of a pastoral associate. A pastoral associate is someone who has some theological training, and assists the parish priest with administering to the pastoral needs of the parish by doing most of the things an assistant priest may have done back in the day. Although the role is sometimes filled by nuns, it is mostly filled by a lay person, and most pastoral associates are women.

By the late noughties, it was becoming apparent that the Church hierarchy was becoming increasingly less tolerant of progressive views within the church.

Our crime this time was that we were overtly promoting progressive views, not always using the proper words during services, and occasionally allowing lay people to speak during homilies. It was hard to know where the complaints were coming from, but it is suspected that once our foibles came to the attention of the Archdiocese, people from outside the parish would come to our services and take notes. Such people are referred to as the Temple Police. They get this moniker because they take note of indiscretions and report them both to the Archdiocese and the Vatican. By including the Vatican in their reports, they ensure a response from the Archdiocese. The fact that we had well-attended services with an engaged congregation did not influence their decision to put our parish on the naughty list.

The upshot of this intervention was that our parish priest was moved on and, just prior to the appointment of a new parish priest, the Archdiocese informed our pastoral associate that her services were no longer required.

Upon receiving this news, I and a few other concerned parishioners wrote to the Archbishop to challenge this assessment. Astonishingly, it appears that as soon as our letters hit the Archbishop's desk, a response was drafted. The response stated that the decision had been made by the new parish priest, and we were reminded that pastoral councillors did not have any authority within the Parish and were only there to provide advice to the parish priest. In my letter, I did not identify myself as a pastoral councillor, but somehow, they knew.

Not satisfied with this response, we resolved that we would address the congregations at the forthcoming Sunday services to inform them of what was going on. Word of this must have reached the Archdiocese because ten minutes before the first service was due to begin, our pastoral associate got a call from the new parish priest (who was still a couple of weeks off from commencing his new appointment) asking her to stay on. Despite this, we went ahead with our planned address to the congregations.

This experience left me in no doubt that conservative forces had assumed control of the church and were bending over backwards to stifle any progressive thought and would reverse all the 2nd Vatican Council reforms if they could.

Our Parish was never the same after that. The new parish priest provided absolutely zero spiritual inspiration and was only there to provide the doctrinal needs of the Catholic Church. After receiving numerous abusive letters and emails from various sources, our pastoral associate decided to move on. I too, decided that I couldn't continue in my role as a pastoral councillor and resumed a passive role in the church congregation like most other Catholics. I did, however, channel my experiences into my satirical novel, *Pope Dreams: Pope Peter The Improbable*, which was published at the end of 2022.

***

So, given the experience described above, am I deluded in thinking that I can still identify as a Roman Catholic?

In my novel, I openly profess that most bishops and cardinals are regressive tossers who support doctrines that are oppressive to women and minority groups. But the basis of my spiritual identity goes back to my experiences with enlightened people within the church itself. I am enthused that the current Pope has been able to push back against some of the more regressive influences within his curia. But I fear that his tenure is just a short reprieve before conservatives again take control. These conservatives seem to admire what Islam has done with religious fundamentalism and relish the idea of doctrinal control of society.

But, like all fundamentalists, they refuse to accept the reality that most of their followers are not religious zealots. Their connection to the church is purely cultural. Doctrinal stances on birth control, abortion, same-sex relationships, and pre-marital sex, are largely ignored. So, the only real future for the church is to become more relevant to the community at large.

I also believe in a form of religious fundamentalism. But my concept of religious fundamentalism is that all faiths return to the fundamental beliefs which formed their religions in the first place. Those fundamental beliefs are that all living things and the universe around us are inextricably connected, such that whatever we do to harm any element of our world harms all of us. All indigenous cultures share this belief system in one form or another. This is what I like to call true religious fundamentalism. People can continue to gather and worship within the faith that aligns with their culture. But everyone accepts that our individual belief systems have the same basis.

***

So, I live in hope of true reform within the Catholic Church. I know that I am not alone in this pursuit. In fact, in my experience, most people active in the church are of the view that the church needs to evolve to maintain its relevance in the modern world. But this involves breaking another doctrinal taboo: interpreting the words in the Bible relative to the societal norms of our times. Such relativism, however, engenders apoplectic fits of rage within most traditional bishops and cardinals. They are still holding on to the 15th Century views, that individuals should not be permitted to interpret scripture in a form that is relative to their current existence. But they believe in God as a supernatural puppet master, and we all know that such a being does not exist.

So, how compatible is my belief system with traditional Christian doctrine? In order to assess this, I thought that I should have a look at the Nicene Creed and do a bit of a comparison. For those unfamiliar with it, the Nicene Creed is common to all Christian churches. It was developed by the early Christian leaders in the year 325CE and aims to set out the rules of what it means to be Christian. It is commonly recited during the Catholic Mass, and I believe it is recited during the services of other denominations as well. My comparison between the Nicene Creed and my beliefs is set out below:

Nicene Creed	Stephen's Take
We believe in one God, the Father, the Almighty, Maker of heaven and earth, of all that is seen and unseen.	God = Life, the universe and everything.

Nicene Creed	Stephen's Take
We believe in one Lord Jesus Christ, the only Son of God, eternally begotten of the Father; God from God, Light from Light, true God from true God; begotten not made, one in being with the Father. Through Him all things were made.	Jesus = God in human form = Us
For us men and for our salvation He came down from heaven. By the power of the Holy Spirit, He was born of the Virgin Mary and became man.	Jesus had a mother and was a human being.
For our sake He was crucified under Pontius Pilate. He suffered, died, and was buried.	Jesus was sentenced to death for being a threat to the powers that be, and that sentence was carried out.
On the third day He rose again, in fulfillment of the Scriptures.	Although this one man died, what he stood for lives on in all of us.

He ascended into heaven and is seated at the right hand of the Father.	On his death, his spirit became one with the universe again (as will ours).
He will come again in glory to judge the living and the dead, and His kingdom will have no end.	We are the eternal embodiment of Jesus.
We believe in the Holy Spirit, the Lord, the Giver of life, who proceeds from the Father and the Son. With the Father and the Son, He is worshipped and glorified. He has spoken through the prophets.	We are bound to the universe by an inexplicable force. This force is within all of us and can be harnessed to provide guidance and help us to be our best selves.
We believe in one, holy, catholic, and apostolic Church.	All religions have equal standing, and we all have a responsibility to spread the faith.
We acknowledge one baptism for the forgiveness of sins. We look for the resurrection of the dead and the life of the world to come.	We acknowledge our spiritual connectivity and take comfort in the knowledge that our spirits will live on when we leave our mortal bodies.

It is impossible for me to know if the delegates at the First Council of Nicaea in 325CE shared my sentiments, but I really don't think that I am far off. A literal interpretation of the Creed requires one to consider Jesus Christ as a supernatural being, whereas the Gospels go to great lengths to describe Jesus as a human being who espoused a way of life that provided care and respect for everyone and everything. So, the miracle of the resurrection is not that one man was able to cheat death, but that what that man stood for is able to live on for over 2000 years.

This organic view of Christianity is out of step with the doctrinal view of a puppet-master God and a faith-healing messiah. But to me, the whole story of Jesus doesn't make sense unless Jesus was 100% human. How else are we to live up to his standard?

Still

Liz Reichard

'In case no one told you today, you're special.'

From the song *Special* by Lizzo

I grew up walking on eggshells. My father was volatile, with a searing rage that would start over the smallest thing. Scented shampoo? Off he went. His dinner wasn't hot enough? Yep, off again. He woke up feeling crap? Oh yeah, you knew that was going to be a shit day.

As a child, I tried to toe the line, be a good girl, do what I was told and try to keep him happy. It didn't work, of course, because, in hindsight, I don't think anything would have. He was the product of World War II, a child enlisted in the German Air Force. He learned how to fly, and that was his greatest joy, although I don't think he ever did it again after the war. He was taken prisoner of war by the Canadians and then held in a camp by the British.

He had his 18th birthday in that prisoner-of-war camp and had 18 peas in his soup. I don't know much about what happened during the war; he would have his set stories he would tell, about ten or so, and that was it. It was only much later that I realised that we only heard the 'light' stories, nothing heavier or of real substance. He'd have been diagnosed with PTSD now. But back then such things weren't really known, and by the time they were, there would have been no way he'd have gone to get help.

As I grew up, I started to push back. I yelled back at him, refused to listen to his ranting anymore and plotted my escape. Those teenage years are never fun, but I reckon it's a lot harder when you've got someone who seems to be actively trying to tear you down, all the while saying he's trying to help. It was a frequent line of attack that if I didn't do well at school, I'd end up as a prostitute. Lord only knows how he managed to make that jump - Macca's employee, maybe but a hooker? It was meant to urge me to work harder, which it did to a certain extent, but it also ate into my spirit and my self-esteem. It made me doubt my own abilities even while trying to prove him wrong. Talk about conflicting emotions!

I remember that he always told me I could become the first female Prime Minister. I remember when I was about seven talking to him about this and trying to work out what I would need to do to make it happen. I don't remember the exact words, but I know that he suggested I become a lawyer as a first step. And so the seed was planted. I was going to be a lawyer. Looking back now, I reckon my entire subsequent legal career was to make him happy. And I'm not even sure it did.

But I looked after that little seed, made sure it had enough water and sunlight, and it grew. It grew and grew, and I grew with it; leaning into this idea that I would be a lawyer who would help people. And I did. I worked through high school, but I didn't quite make the grades I needed. I enrolled in another degree and, worked harder, and got marks that meant I was accepted into a law degree later on. I pushed harder again, raising a baby, working four jobs, studying and trying to have a social life.

Finally, I finished and then... nothing. For a full 12 months, I couldn't find a paid job. So I changed tack, and I found work experience at a community legal centre instead. I worked there for about six months, and then once I was qualified, they offered me a job! I was off and running, seemingly happy, having finally reached my goal.

I was helping people who didn't have the skills or funds to solve their legal problems. I was working with many women who were in the very worst situations of their lives. I was doing good work. I stayed in the industry for about ten years, working at various organisations, trying to keep up the good fight. It worked for a while, but I could feel myself burning out. It's hard to keep pushing every day to help your clients who are often in the most horrific circumstances without adequate support in place for your own mental health.

The spirit was waning; it wasn't right. I'm not sure that it had ever been right, if that seed was ever really meant to be mine to water. But without it, I doubt I would have found my true spirit. The one I'm meant to nurture and grow with, embrace and carry through the rest of my life.

The start of the change in me came with the death of my father in December 2011. Finally, I could stop walking on eggshells; I could relax at home. I never realised what a privilege it was to feel safe and relaxed in your own home until I finally experienced it for myself. It also highlighted how bad things really had been: the paranoia, the rage, the impossible expectations I had navigated for the past 31 years of my life. The fear I had felt, the energy used to push back, keep quiet or just leave for the evening. Suddenly there was no more need for it.

In the last five or so years of his life, I had been a regular at our local pub - and I mean regular - at least twice a week. I was going out to avoid being at home with him. And I was drinking A LOT. So much so, I was concerned I might have a drinking problem. To check, I did FebFast in 2012. FebFast is a month-long challenge to raise money for disadvantaged youth by abstaining from alcohol. I passed with flying colours. I was able to stop drinking overnight. And I found that I no longer wanted to go to the pub. I realised how I had structured my life to try and avoid being at home with him, and to be honest, I was devastated. I didn't go out to enjoy other people's company and have fun; I went out to give myself a break from being hyper-vigilant.

I started to notice other things about myself now that I could finally breathe. I realised that my career wasn't making me happy and that I needed a change. I quit my job, took ten months off then found a new gig. I thought that I was happy, but it was short-lived. My spirit was looking for something else, but I didn't know yet what it was.

Then I had a mental health breakdown and had to go on to Workcover. I shattered like a mirror, and my entire career was blown into smithereens. I sought help from my GP, a psychologist and a psychiatrist. I followed their advice, changed my medication, went for walks and tried to deal with my past traumas. Slowly I started to feel better, but it was very, very small baby steps.

I found a post on Facebook advertising a day-long retreat in Macedon. There was meditation, yoga, free writing and this thing called Qoya. I had never heard of it, and the description seemed vague. I didn't think much of it at the time, but boy, was it about to change my life in a billion different ways!

The Qoya teacher, now a dear friend, Nicola Belcher, came from Melbourne for the session. She introduced it as, 'A movement practice based on the idea that through movement, we remember. We remember that our essence is Wise, Wild and Free. There are no levels in Qoya, and no way to do it wrong. The way you know you are doing it right; is that it feels good to you. It feels true. It feels honest.'

We started moving, being guided by Nicola's directions. It felt so good not to worry about what my movements looked like and instead focus on the feeling. To feel into my body after years of being up in my head. To really allow myself to feel my emotions and to dance with them. I saw other women also having profound breakthroughs during the class, crying hysterically over emotions they had long kept buried. It was unlike any other class I had ever been to. I knew this was something special, and I was glad to have experienced it. I looked into going to Nicola's classes, but they were in Richmond, a good hour-plus drive from my home, and it was too much for me at that time.

I knew that I could never go back to being a lawyer again. My heart was no longer in it, and I shuddered at the thought of practicing law again. At the same time, I was excited. It was time for me to work out what I wanted my seed to be, where I wanted to take my life. As if I had a choice for the first time that was truly mine. I knew what I didn't want anymore, and now it was time to work out what it was that I did want, like a kid in a lolly shop trying to work out what they truly want to buy with their dollar. What did I want to do with my life? My son and I went for a long walk and started talking about what I could do next. We were spitballing, throwing around wild ideas of what I could do with my life. Invent something? Make something? But in the end, we didn't come close to any sort of an answer.

I then saw that there was an upcoming wellbeing festival at the Abbotsford Convent in April 2019 called Superbloom, and Nicola was going to be leading Qoya there! I recruited a friend and went along for the day. I went to the Qoya class by myself; my friend had another session she really wanted to go to.

I entered the huge room, which had a wooden floor and yoga mats laid out in a circle. There was an altar of candles, oracle cards and flowers in the centre. It looked so lovely and inviting. I sat down and eagerly waited for the class to start. The theme was *Bloom*, to fit in with the name of the festival. I wish I could remember more of the actual class itself, but all I can recall is this feeling of wonder and joy at having experienced Qoya again.

At the end of the class, we were invited to share with the person next to us about the class. Unbeknownst to me, the blonde curly-haired woman I turned to was also a Qoya teacher. She asked me what I thought about the class, and I told her, 'Oh, it's just wonderful. I love it.' What she said next changed the course of my life forever (or maybe this is what it was always meant to be?). She said, 'Why don't you teach?' Her words hit me like Marie Kondo's spark joy - THIS IS WHAT I WAS MEANT TO DO!

After the class was over, I excitedly met up with my friend again and, bursting with joy, told her I was going to become a Qoya teacher. She didn't quite share my enthusiasm, but then she hadn't felt the lightning bolt I had! I felt as if I had finally found the real reason why I was put on this earth. My spirit was ignited in a way it had never, ever been before. Still buzzing, I went home and told my mum and son that I had found my calling and that it was Qoya. They have supported me fully and wholly from that day onwards in my quest to become a Qoya teacher and beyond.

I made the commitment to go to Nicola's fortnightly classes, and found that the more I danced with my feelings rather than thought about them, the better I felt. Each class made me more and more sure that this was what I was meant to be doing. I spoke to Nicola about the teacher training and found the website for it. The training was broken up into three parts, the first online and the second two in person. The training wasn't cheap, and I was only receiving Workcover payments. The closest in-person training was in New Zealand. I decided I would do part 1 and see if it really was for me before committing to the rest of it.

What happened next proved to me that I was being supported by the universe and that I was right to follow my heart to become a Qoya teacher. A dear friend of mine offered to pay for the first part of the training as my 40th birthday present. My son won a decent chunk of cash on a game show and secretly put $1,000 into my bank account, which I used to go to New Zealand for Part 2. My mum offered to pay for Part 3 for me. It was a case of jump, and you will be caught. Everything was lining up for me to become a Qoya teacher.

Once I started the training, I knew I was on the right track. My whole body was saying YES to Qoya. I was excited, lit up and engaged in a way I hadn't been for a very long time, maybe in a way that I had never been before. Each step I took, each module I studied, each class I danced, made me more and more certain that I was on the right track.

The trip to New Zealand in October 2019 for Part 2 cemented it for me. It was a weekend-long training with six other women, and it was incredible. We explored each part of a class in depth, with the teacher pushing us to look deeper, feel more and see what we would find. I cried, I laughed, and I made friends. I was sure I was in the right place.

After Part 2, I had to teach 11 practice classes for friends and family before I could do Part 3. I intended to go back to New Zealand for Part 3 in October 2020. But as you might recall, 2020 had its own ideas on what was going to happen! For me, it ended up being a blessing of sorts.

Suddenly, because I was using Zoom for my classes, I could invite friends who were interstate or overseas. I flew through my 11 practice classes and hoped against hope that the border between Australia and New Zealand would open in time for Part 3. Sadly, it wasn't to be, so instead, I transferred my enrolment to the online course. The online course was with Rochelle Schieck, the founder of Qoya. Now Rochelle lives in New York State, so this was not going to be an easy task.

For three days, I studied online from 1 am to 3 am and then from 6 am to 9 am. For the other four, I was online from 6 am to 9 am. You haven't lived until you've taught a Qoya class at 1 am!! But I did it, and I was finally a fully qualified Qoya teacher!

For me, becoming a Qoya teacher was not just about finding what lit me up or even the dancing. It was a way that I could continue to help women, albeit in a very different way from when I was still practicing law. It was about empowering them, showing them, and helping them realise how wonderful, strong and powerful they are. That they have all of it inside them already, they just need to find it, tap into it and use it. To remember that their essence, their spirit, is inherently Wise, Wild and Free.

It's also a way for me to provide a safe space, where each woman can come as she is, without judgement or shame. Where she can share how she feels and is supported by the other women in the circle. Women used to gather in circles to prepare food, weave, share stories, drum, sing and dance. They had a community they could go to when they needed help. Sadly, for the most part, we've lost that. My dream is to build a community for the women who come to my classes.

Each time I dance Qoya, I marvel at the simplicity of noticing what an emotion feels like in your body and then dancing with it. With both the shadow and the light, shaking out what no longer serves you. The joy of the free dance, being able to be wildly, truly myself. The lightness in my heart, my soul, and my spirit that I get to share this incredible class with other women.

I strongly believe that Qoya helped me recover much faster from my breakdown - or should that be breakthrough? - than if I hadn't found it. Not just because it gave me a renewed focus for my life, but because of the remembering I felt in my body. I think that every person should have an embodiment practice in their self-care toolkit, be it yoga, hiking or Qoya. Because if I hadn't found Qoya, I'd still be spinning in my head, over-thinking about my emotions and not knowing how to deal with them. With Qoya, I've been able to process some of them (there are still heaps to go!) through moving with them and then shaking it all out.

Thinking that the worst of the pandemic was behind us by the end of 2020, full of hope and enthusiasm, I started my business Sunranges Qoya in January 2021. I held my first-ever class on 1 February 2021 in Fitzroy North. In that first week, I taught five classes. Things were looking great! And then 2021 looked at 2020 and said, 'Here hold my beer!' and Melbourne went on to become the most locked-down city in the world that year. Not great for a brand new business that was mainly leading in-person dance classes!

But I am still here. Still dancing one class at a time. Still feeling that this business will grow and support me financially. Still positive that I am meant to be bringing Qoya to as many women as I can. Still sure that this is what I am meant to be doing with my life. Still sure that this is what my spirit within needs.

An Unexplained Knowing

Lesley Lennon

Listen to the voice inside your head. Notice and interpret the feelings in your gut and heart. Together these are your spirit within communicating with you and guiding you along life's journey.

Lesley Lennon

My name is Lesley. I am the youngest of three daughters. I was born two months earlier than expected in the winter of 1965. As far back as I can recall, I distinctly sensed there was more to the world than what I could see. It was a feeling I could not explain, but it was something I knew deep within my core. This is what I now call my 'spirit within'.

As I grew, it became clear I could not, without ridicule or judgment, share my ideas with my parents or siblings. My parents, in their own words, were 'atheists' and expressed no tolerance for anyone who claimed to have spiritual or religious insight. My father referred to anyone who voiced differing beliefs from his own as being, 'not right in the head.' This statement brought me great fear. I kept my beliefs to myself. Despite the repercussions Dad implied, a voice in my head continued to say, 'You're wrong, Dad. I know there is more.'

To openly express my thoughts, I knew, could lead to admonishment from the family. When I was seven years old, and my eldest sister was 16, I witnessed her being told to, 'Get out' by my father and to, 'Find herself somewhere else to live.' This occurred after many family arguments involving my mother, father, and middle sister. I can remember thinking, 'How can you do this to a child you are supposed to love?' The reasons for her departure were not religious in nature, but from what I was told were because she wanted to go out with a boy who wore his hair 'long'. Remembering the fashion of the 70s, I think most boys of the time wore their hair that way. For me, her exile from the family and the reason given made no sense.

Now I see there may have been more to the situation than I was privy to but at the age of seven, my fear of losing the only family I had was high. Mum and Dad's families of origin both lived in Adelaide, and we lived in Melbourne. Though the geographical distance was not great, we had very little to do with Mum's side of the family and nothing to do with Dad's. I knew I too, could end up like my sister if I didn't, 'toe the line' and pretend to agree with Dad.

At varying times in my life, I have craved to learn more about my 'spirit within'. The intensity to learn has increased during times of adversity and challenge. Such times have included: during my early childhood and adolescence, when preparing for marriage, while raising my children, and bereavement after the passing of both my parents, as well as during the 2020 Covid19 pandemic.

Throughout this time, I have developed and strengthened the understanding that God and the spirit world can communicate with us. This knowledge has served to bring me a sense of comfort. My learning has drawn me toward the guidance of clairvoyants, numerologists, and tarot card readers, who I believe can communicate with the spirit world. Through them, I have discovered how communication can take place. It has made me look not only within myself but around me for physical signs and synchronicities. Now I believe everything happens for a reason.

In my early 20s, when I was at the beginning of my spiritual journey, I remember feeling as though I needed to find a religion to follow. I felt I needed to publicly worship God if my connection with him was to grow. I desperately wanted to find a safe place where I could express my belief with other like-minded people. I wanted a sense of belonging, a sense I didn't have within my own family. I didn't know where to begin looking for my special place, but I sensed within myself that God would guide me in the right direction.

The idea of following a religion was foreign to me. At the time, I was only aware of three religions, and I desperately wanted to know more about each one. I wanted to choose the right one for me. My knowledge was based purely on the people who were around me at school, at home or in my community. The Jehovah's Witness, Catholic, and The Church of England were the main religions I was aware of. Most people I knew were Catholic. When I asked, 'What's the difference between each?', no one could tell me. They would answer, 'The Catholic and Church of

England religions are similar whilst The Jehovah's Witnesses religion is very different'. Everyone I spoke to implied that being a Catholic was by far the best religion to follow.

I thought that maybe they were right. I didn't know anything about Jehovah's Witnesses, but I did remember seeing them in my neighbourhood when I was about seven years old. They would gather in pairs, usually a man and a woman, each with their hair neatly combed and wearing a smart suit. Both stood out as they held either a bunch of pamphlets or a satchel. I knew they knocked on people's doors to deliver what they called, 'The Good News.' We were always told to 'run' and hide whenever Mum saw them approach our house. To say they stood out was an understatement. Mum and Dad always described them as 'nutters'.

Growing up in the 70s, it seemed to me anyone who felt pressure to say they had a religious belief but didn't, said they were a Church of England follower. My mum fell into this category, though never when Dad was around. I longed to ask Mum why she did this but knew my questions would go unanswered.

Throughout my childhood, when the topic of religion or spirituality came up, Dad always appeared uncomfortable, angry, and argumentative. His body would become rigid, his voice loud and aggressive, and he would demand to be shown evidence God existed. His reaction was totally different from my own. I didn't need to question God's existence or know all the answers. I just knew in my heart that God existed, and that was enough for me.

I understood Dad's negative view was centred on his experience as a child. When he was five years old, my grandmother remarried, and Dad was sent to a Catholic orphanage for the length of her honeymoon. Dad rarely spoke about his experience there, but I knew from his behaviour it was an unpleasant time for him. 'Bloody hypocrites' he would call anyone associated with religion.

My father thought religion and spirituality were one and the same. The concept of there being more to life than what he could see or explain was ridiculous to him. His point of view always made me feel sad. I thought, 'Dad, if only you knew what you were missing out on.' I knew having faith in God could bring comfort and take away the anxiety of always needing to be in control. I think Dad's life and my childhood would have been vastly different if Dad had held this view.

Throughout my youth, I came across many people who said they were Catholic. Initially, I did not know what being Catholic meant. My first real introduction to Catholicism came at the age of 18 when I met Steve.

I was in my final year of High School, and he was returning to school after leaving the previous year to find work. Before leaving, Steve and I had been at the same school for several years, so it seemed odd we hadn't seen each other before. I guess the time, in God's view, wasn't yet right.

When Steve returned to school in 1983, the girls in my year level asked me, 'Have you met Steve yet?' We hadn't met until one lunchtime when we crossed paths for the first time. It was a strange introduction and one that felt very much guided by the divine. You see, on this day, I decided to join a year 12 basketball game. That may not seem surprising, but I had never before joined in on any school sports. In primary school, I played sport and wasn't too bad at it, but at high school, I was never brave enough to have a go. For some reason, on this day, something was different.

As it happened, when I started playing the game, I was still munching on my half-eaten apple from lunch, and uncharacteristically, I decided to throw it away. To my embarrassment, it hit Steve, and that is when our first interaction took place. The situation was weird because I was always known as a 'goodie goodie' and never broke the school rules. To throw the apple anywhere other than into a bin was totally out of character.

Before meeting Steve, fitting in at school or anywhere, for that matter, was difficult. I put it down to the nomadic lifestyle my family lived. Until I was 12 years old, my father was a retail store manager. Dad's job made us move house every 12 to 18 months. We would move from suburb to suburb in Melbourne, Regional Victoria, and interstate. This made it difficult for us to make lasting friendships or have a sense of community. I found it difficult to trust people. I lacked confidence and presented as shy and withdrawn.

At the same time, power struggles at home between my two elder sisters were common, and arguments were regular. For the most part, I hid as best I could. I felt different from the rest of my family and as though I wasn't related to them. I felt alone and lost. My only solace was to talk to God, 'Please God, help me.' I couldn't see God, but I knew he was there.

Starting a new school was difficult. Each time I started a new school, I did it alone. Both my sisters were older than me by five, and nine years. I would often arrive mid-year when friendships and hierarchies were already established. On occasion, I found the children to be cruel and unaccepting. Adding to this, Mum and Dad insisted I wear my hair in long, tightly braided plaits, each with enormous bows hanging from them. I knew I looked different. Sometimes the kids would say, 'Take your hair out,' and to gain friendships, I did. At the end of the day, when I returned home with my hair freely flowing, all hell would break loose.

At home, the evenings and weekends were even worse. My parents argued incessantly, and alcohol played its part in fuelling them. Dad frequently lost his temper, and Mum would bear the brunt of a fist or backhand. When this happened, I would cover my hands over my ears to block the sound of Mum's cries, lock myself in my room and eventually cry myself to sleep.

The next morning the damage would be evident, but the pretence that everything was normal continued. On a school day, Dad would have left for work by the time I got up to go to school. Mum would be in the kitchen making our school lunches wearing sunglasses to cover her blackened and bloodshot eyes. Her thighs would be hidden under her slacks, and I knew they too, would be battered and bruised. No words were ever spoken about the events of the night before.

To get to school, I either walked or took the bus. On many occasions, I wanted to tell someone what I was going through. The fear of being sent to a children's home stopped me. it was a place Mum and Dad often threatened to send us if ever we were naughty or misbehaved. I was always afraid. The only thing that calmed me was praying to God. He listened and gave me the strength and determination to 'keep going.' There were many times when I didn't think I could.

By the time I started high school, the theme of wanting to connect with someone and find my place of belonging was strong. 'Please God,' I'd say, 'Find me someone to love who will love me in return.' So, when Steve and I met at school and formed a relationship, I read this as a sign from God. I had been out with other boys, but Steve was different.

Not long after Steve and I began to date, I learned he was Catholic, and, to me, this was yet another sign from God. I felt sure God wanted me to learn more about the Catholic faith. However, as our relationship progressed, it became clear that Steve's family were not devout Catholics and only attended church at Christmas time. Nonetheless, I thought, 'Maybe I have found the sense of belonging I have been looking for.' I hoped going to Christmas Mass would help to create happy family memories and experiences, especially for the family Steve and I dreamed of having in the future.

In the beginning, I found going to Church challenging. I didn't know what to say or when. I was confused by the rituals and struggled to follow those around me. I did, however, enjoy being with other people who shared a belief in God. I was no longer alone. I thought God had brought me to a place where I was meant to be. It made sense two years after leaving school for Steve and me to get married in a Catholic Church. My parents were not thrilled by our decision, with Dad saying, 'I'm not bowing down to any so-called God.'

Despite being married in a Church of England Cathedral in 1952, Dad had no desire to be in a church, let alone participate in any of its sacraments. It took some persuading and stipulations before Mum and Dad agreed to attend the wedding. Dad said, 'There will be no Mass, kneeling or bowing.'

Once the decision to marry was made, Steve and I set out to find a Catholic church to be married in. It wasn't an easy task. It took many hours of door-knocking before we found a priest who was willing to even think about marrying us. Neither of us belonged to a parish, and so we needed to prove we were worthy of being married in the Catholic Church.

'Surely,' I thought, 'A priest can see we are good people with good intentions.' To prove our worthiness, we were asked to attend premarital classes. The priest said, 'You will need to show your commitment and understanding of the Catholic faith.'

Although I was happy to have found a Catholic priest who would potentially marry us, my stomach was twisting and turning. I kept thinking, 'What if we don't get the approval?' At the time, it seemed there was no alternative other than to be married in a Catholic church. Now, in hindsight, I can think of so many alternatives. Maybe God was guiding me along this path for a reason.

When the weekend for the first of the three premarital sessions arrived, I was anxious. The sessions took place in a Catholic church on the grounds of an exclusive private boys' school in the Eastern suburbs. When we arrived, we were surrounded by opulent houses, buildings, and religious monuments. We were not accustomed to such wealth. It made me feel uncomfortable and as though we didn't belong. The desire to leave and go home was strong. I could sense God saying, 'Follow the journey,' and so we stayed.

I took Steve's hand tightly and entered the church. Reaching the altar seemed to take forever. It was only then we noticed the priest. He sat rigid in his chair, almost like a statue. When he did move, he called out to us, 'Are you two here for the premarital sessions?' His face held no warmth or friendliness as he spoke. We both timidly nodded in response as he continued to point to some papers on the altar. 'Fill out the questionnaire and sign in sheet and give it to me!' he yelled.

With shaky hands, we both began to fill out our forms. Instantly I felt clammy, and the voice in my head kept saying, 'I don't know what to do here. I feel so out of place.' I was worried about admitting the truth. I hadn't been baptised and had no religious background. I sensed this news wouldn't be received well. I quickly read the questionnaire, and sure enough, it asked, 'Where were you baptised?' And 'If you are not Catholic, what religion do you belong to?'

I felt panicked and left the questions unanswered. I returned the papers to the priest and moved as quickly as I could to my seat. I hoped he wouldn't notice the blank spaces, but before I knew what was happening, he shouted, 'If you are not Catholic, what religion are you?' Automatically I did just as my mum had done and said, 'Church of England.' 'Well,' he said, 'You had better concentrate because you have a lot to learn.'

Instantly I felt upset and uncomfortable. His behaviour towards me was cold and unfriendly. His clothes of black pants and jumper, white shirt, and clerical collar lacked personality. I felt as though I was looking at a clone. The God I knew in my heart represented love, acceptance, and individuality. This man represented none of those things. I couldn't wait for the sessions to end and was elated three weeks later when we received our permission to marry. Steve and I married in November 1985.

In the early years of our marriage, Steve and I continued the tradition of attending church for Christmas and later also for Easter celebrations. Despite my initial enjoyment during these times, my discomfort in the presence of the priests continued. They were not approachable, and I had no understanding of the religion I was trying to follow. I felt like a sheep blindly following the flock.

I justified my Catholic worshipping by saying to myself, 'Priests have a closer relationship with God than me.' I saw them as extensions of God, and as people I needed to help me build my relationship with him. This idea was also strongly conveyed by the Catholic community. At the same time, my intuition was saying, 'Pray to God anywhere at any time, and he will hear you. Talk to him directly, and he will listen, support, and guide you.' The two thoughts conflicted, and I felt confused. Adding to my dilemma was the need to choose a school for our daughter, who was soon approaching school age.

The pressure I placed on myself to make the right decision was high. Negative childhood memories of being the 'new kid' were vivid in my mind. I didn't want my daughter to begin her school life in one school only to change to another. Neither Steve nor I could decide which education would be better: a Catholic School or a state school. We both knew we wanted her to have a spiritual education. I knew she would receive a predominantly religious education in a Catholic school and would, with our permission, receive a little religious instruction in a state school.

Steve's family was convinced a Catholic education would be best. They felt regret for not sending their own children to a Catholic school. I was confused and prayed to God, 'Please give me the answer.'

Within days an answer came knocking on my door. A smartly dressed middle-aged woman arrived with her daughter. She introduced herself as Julie and her daughter as Claire. They both, she explained, were from the Jehovah's Witnesses and asked, 'Can we come in and chat with you?' Given my history, you would have expected me to say, 'No!' but for some reason, I said 'Yes', and they both came into my home.

Straight away, I felt a connection with Julie and Claire. As I watched them interact with each other, I could feel their genuine love, respect, and closeness. I thought this may have been because of the religion they both represented. I wanted to have the same relationship with my children. They gained my attention and intrigue. We continued to meet for several months.

As time went by, I began to feel as though I may have found my spiritual home. I shared my experiences and teachings with Steve. Soon he too was keen to learn more, and before long, we were socialising with Julie's family and attending their Church. We realised we didn't fully align with all aspects of their religion, but the sense of openness, belonging and willingness to answer our questions pulled us towards them.

As we became more and more drawn to the religion, we thought it best to share our experiences with Steve's family. I was too afraid to mention anything to my own family. Our enthusiasm was soon dampened and met with great disdain. 'Jehovah's Witnesses don't celebrate Christmas or birthdays,' they argued. 'We love Christmas. You cannot join them!'

That was pretty much that. Shortly after this reaction, we stopped seeing our friends from the Jehovah's Witnesses or attending their Church. When the time came to choose a school for our daughter, we chose the local Catholic primary school. It was a decision I wasn't comfortable with, but I hoped her own 'spirit within' would guide her. My parents, though not thrilled, accepted our decision so long as we never asked them to attend church with us.

Returning to the Catholic faith left me for many years feeling empty and as though something was missing. Whilst our children attended Catholic Primary School, I felt pretentious and hypocritical. Over the years, I improved my ability to follow the flock by kneeling at the right times, saying the responses on cue and shaking hands whilst saying: 'Peace be with you,' but there was no feeling in my actions. I didn't understand what I was doing or saying.

By this time, we had three children, and I thought if we were to send all three to a Catholic School, I needed to have a better understanding of what they were being taught. Priests were still unapproachable and unwilling to answer my questions. I didn't know how I could learn more. 'Please God, tell me what to do,' I prayed.

The response again came shortly after my prayer and occurred while I was in Sunday Mass. When reading the Parish newsletter, I saw the words, 'Anyone wanting to learn more about Our Lord Jesus Christ, contact June on this number.' This is no coincidence, I thought. 'God has given me a sign.'

Later that week, as instructed, I made the call and arranged for June to come to our home. On the evening of her arrival, I was anxious and unsure of what to expect. When the doorbell rang, I hurried to open the door. What I saw was a robust elderly woman. She was not Julie by any means, and the kinship I had instantly felt with Julie was not there. Putting aside my initial disappointment, my intuition told me to 'keep going with the lessons.'

The lessons ran for many months. Throughout the lessons, I continued to question my alignment with Catholic beliefs. However, to mark the end of the lessons, I was baptised Catholic. Again, despite my questions, I sensed God was telling me it was the right thing for me to do. At the time, I felt I was showing my reverence to God, and now I see baptism as an expression of respect and love for God regardless of the religion.

In the years that followed, our children continued to attend both Catholic primary and secondary schools. All the while, I remained an active member of the

Catholic community by both attending and preparing the Church each Sunday for Mass. With each passing year though, my desire to attend church lessened to the point I stopped going altogether.

It's been 16 years since I last attended a Catholic church to pray. I have at times, missed the sense of belonging that worshipping in this way brings. Today, though, I am content to pray to God as I did as a child: privately and without the guidance or interception of a priest. I continue to believe my 'spirit within' is my guide and connection to God and the spirit world.

After researching and reading about spirituality, I have become aware of the many ways the spirit world has attempted to connect and communicate with me. I now believe everything happens for a reason, and nothing is a coincidence. One example of this is the passing of my father on my 41st birthday. While alive, Dad and I were never close. The reasons were many and varied. My belief in God and the spirit world was just one opposing view we both held.

In passing away on my birthday, I imagine Dad was attempting to tell me I was right about my beliefs. I trust he wanted to further prove his point and gain my attention by influencing some unexplainable incidents to take place. For example, during the week following my father's death, both my mother's television and grandfather clock randomly stopped and started without anyone touching them. Dad's car also would not start until a mechanic was called, at which time it started on the first attempt. I can see Dad laughing from above as we tried to make sense of these incidents.

When Mum passed away in 2020, similar signs and synchronicities occurred. The timing of Mum's death in the May of 2020 almost seemed to be planned. At that time, the impact of the Covid19 Pandemic had only just begun in Australia. To protect the vulnerable in aged care facilities, a lockdown was put in place. This meant no one was allowed to enter a nursing home to visit a loved one.

These restrictions were enforced for many months as the virus continued to spread within the community. Oddly, or through what I call divine intervention, the restrictions were lifted the week prior to Mum passing away. In thinking about this, I feel as though the spirit world played its part in allowing Mum and me to say our last goodbye. The opportunity to see Mum one last time provided me with a treasured memory of us both laughing and chatting together. Strangely, the following week the restrictions were put back in place.

Divine intervention, I sense, also played its part in the actual time of Mum's death. Mum passed away at 7.30pm on a Friday evening. It was a time that allowed my family and I to come together to support and comfort one another. The evening hour also made it possible for us to enter the home without disturbance. This was very much a characteristic of my mother. She never wanted to be an inconvenience to anyone.

Additionally, I think Mum knew she was going to be taken to hospital and chose to die at home. We would not have been able to travel with her in the ambulance or be with her at the hospital because of the Pandemic restrictions. In the past, Mum had made it clear she despised visiting the doctor and did anything she could to avoid a hospital visit.

Just as I saw spiritual signs after Dad's death, I also saw them after Mum's. On two occasions, I witnessed the presence of two white pigeons. In one instance, they were in my backyard and in another they were many kilometres away in my daughter's backyard. Through research, I have found documentation that suggests birds can be seen as a spiritual sign of a loved one who is deceased. I see the pigeons as a symbol of Mum and Dad letting us know they are now together in the afterlife.

The death of both Mum and Dad has heightened my awareness of spiritual signs around me in my daily life. It is not unusual for me to notice the reoccurrence of numbers in my surroundings. The numbers I commonly see are 8, 11, or 7. Numerologically, each number has its own meaning, but put simply, collectively they are telling me that I need to tune into and listen to my intuition, I am on the right path, and I am on the road to further spiritual awakening.

In a similar way to seeing the numbers in my surroundings, I often see the names or initials of people close to me. I see them on vehicle registration plates, street signs, or billboards. Similarly, it is not surprising for me to hear their name in several songs in succession on the radio. I regard this as the spirit world letting me know these people are thinking of me just as I am thinking of them.

Knowing there is a 'spirit within' that can guide, comfort, and communicate with me brings a sense of calm to my inner being. It encourages me to try not to control the flow of life, but to lean into it and go with it.

Over the years, I have come to recognise some practices which I feel help to enhance and strengthen the presence of spirit in my life. Some of these rituals include: lighting candles, burning essential oils, listening to meditative music, breathing deeply, praying, and taking time to be alone.

I will always be grateful for my 'spirit within' and, for as long as my journey in this lifetime continues, I will seek to learn more and be forever guided by it.

Our Messages

In this final chapter, the co-authors share the three main messages they have shared in their chapters. This acts not only as a summary of what they have written about, but as practical advice you can use to assist you in your own personal journey.

The authors in this book have not started their journey as experts. We are all regular people, overcoming our own difficulties and hurdles, to pursue dreams and goals, and for most of us, perhaps all, this is an ongoing process. Part of that process has been writing about our own spirit within and what that means to each of us.

We hope that in sharing these stories, you will be inspired to pursue your dreams and goals and explore your own inner spirit and discover what that means to you.

Antoinette Pellegrini

❖ **Be true to yourself.** We are all unique, and if we are truly ourselves, and true to our spirit within, then we will forge our own path – there is no need to copy anyone else. Everyone has a different 'why'. It could be a passion, it could be family, but ultimately, perhaps our purpose, our 'why' is to be fully who we are. To be ourselves and live in a way that is true to who we are.

❖ **Be in alignment.** The 'magic' happens when you are in alignment with the spirit within, when your everyday life, actions, choices, feelings, and thoughts align with your inner passion, drive, and spirit. Perhaps this is a description of happiness: when everything is in alignment, and you feel totally at peace with who you are. When your inner spirit matches the external circumstances of your life, then you are truly living the manifestation of who you are.

❖ **Your thoughts matter.** The way you think directly impacts on your health and wellbeing, even changing your body chemistry. How you approach something in life, either from a positive or negative viewpoint, can have a significant impact on the outcome, physically, mentally and emotionally. Your thoughts are energy vibrations that can become matter, so it is very true to say, change your thinking, change your life.

Christine Carmuciano

❖ **Don't compare yourself to others and dull your own shine** because of it or let fear grip you so much that you won't even give something a try. You will find that everyone around you at some point in their life has doubted themselves. The difference is whether you let it stop you in your tracks or you push through regardless.

We are the best people to know what is right for ourselves. So if it feels right within your gut or your intuition is telling you so, then trust it, because it knows best, and it is always the right answer for you. It is only your ego mind or that of others that will cause you to doubt and second guess yourself. Remember that if you tell yourself you can't do something, then you won't; but if you tell yourself you can, then you will!

❖ **Learn to fill your own cup first, it's not selfish!** So many times we put ourselves last; many times to the detriment of our physical and emotional selves. Putting our family and friends first above our own needs, although it comes from a place of love, can actually be an act of self-sabotage and not loving ourselves enough to put our own needs first. Why do we do it? Is it because we think it is our duty; our responsibility? Do we think it will make us a better friend? And then do we resent it when it is not reciprocated? Learning to love yourself enough to say 'no' when you want to say 'no' and 'yes' when you want to say 'yes' is the start of building your self-confidence and knowing your true self.

❖ **Love the skin you're in!** Easier said than done right? Sometimes we are our worst enemy. We wouldn't dare speak to a loved one the way we speak to ourselves in the mirror. I'll try not to preach this one, as it is definitely still a work in progress for me. All I do know is, that if we're able to love ourselves, warts and all, we would walk around lighter and with more joy in our hearts, not only for ourselves but for others too.

Imagine having the freedom and confidence to 'not give a damn'? I'm not saying to be unhealthy; I'm just saying to love ourselves enough that we don't compare ourselves to unrealistic stereotypes or photoshopped pictures in magazines or social media. How can we compare ourselves to something that isn't real right? So why do we do it, even though we know this is the case? Instead let's try to look up to the people that inspire us, deep within our soul, not our materialistic world.

We are more than what we show on Facebook or Instagram or Tik Tok or whatever else is out there for that matter. After all, we're all bound to leave this earth when our time comes, so isn't it far better to focus on what truly matters to us rather than how many 'likes' we get on a post?

Remember that if we're not happy on the inside, then we're not truly happy at all!

Rosalie Carr

- **Be open-minded to the fact that other people have issues too**. You might think that some people have 'cushy' lives, but we don't know what other people are going through. There is no need to judge yourself on what you perceive are other people's lives.

- **Never give up, even when things get tough**. There is always a light at the end of the tunnel, if you look for it. Things can get better. I wasn't going to let my accident define me and stop me from living my life. You can do anything if your spirit within is strong.

- **Forgive those who hurt you, but that doesn't mean you have to keep them in your life**. I am quite content with letting those people go now. Until recently, I felt I had to 'fix' broken relationships and friendships, but now I realise not every person you meet is meant to be in your life forever. I still sometimes find some things hard to forgive, but I have learned that forgiveness is more for yourself, not for the other person/people.

Stephen D'Agata

- **We are spiritual beings temporarily housed in a biological skin**. Intuitively, all spiritual people know that there is more to life than our physical existence. We believe that our spiritual existence preceded our presence on Earth and will survive once we leave this mortal soil. Whatever that spiritual existence is, it is the same for everyone. Despite the beliefs espoused by the leaders of various faith communities, we all came in the same way and we're all going out the same way. There is no heaven, no hell, no purgatory. There is only the universe to which we are inexplicably and inextricably connected.

- **Organised religions rely upon cultural connections to faith to make up their numbers.** The Catholic Church, for example, professes to have one billion followers. One billion! That's 12% of the world population? I however contend, that at least 80% of people who identify as Catholic do so because of their cultural connection to the faith and do not live their lives beholden to the directions of the Pope, Cardinals, and Bishops of the Church. I further contend, that this is true for most faiths. Our cultural ties support our intuitive belief that we are greater than the sum of our parts, but we'll make our own decisions as to what we do with our lives, bodies, and relationships.

❖ **It is possible for universal spirituality to survive within organised religion.** Whatever faith community we belong to or belief system we connect with, the fundamental origins of those communities or systems, are identical. In our short time on this planet, our faiths tell us that we need to be our best selves, look out for others, and care for the delicate environment we call home.

I learnt from Catholic theologians, that the rituals of the Catholic Mass are designed to reinforce our connections with each other and celebrate that we are the body of Christ. Through meditation and prayer, we put ourselves into the bread and wine on the altar and later consume that bread and wine to physically become one with each other. Other faiths have similar rituals that are designed to celebrate our existence as a collective force.

These rituals feed our spiritual needs. So long as we put spirituality ahead of the doctrines, it is possible to satisfy our need to belong to a faith community consistent with our cultural ties and recognise that our culture's path to enlightenment is no greater or lesser than other's cultures.

Lesley Lennon

❖ **Listen to the voice in your head and the feeling in your gut.** It is your intuition and your connection to your 'spirit within'.

❖ **Be open to receiving guidance from your 'spirit within'** and be aware of the ways the spirit world can communicate and connect with you.

❖ **Nothing is a coincidence.** Everything has a reason for happening. We may not always in this lifetime have the opportunity to make sense of each incidence; however, at times, an understanding will be immediate.

Liz Reichard

- **Safety at home is a privilege that not everyone has.** I never realised what a privilege it was to feel safe and relaxed in my own home until I finally could experience it for myself.

- **Find your spark - the thing that lights you up.** Mine was to teach Qoya. When I discovered it, I felt like a lightning bolt had gone through me. I felt as if I had finally found the real reason why I was put on this earth. My spirit was ignited in a way it had never, ever been before. I encourage you to find your spark.

- **Find an activity where you move your body that suits you**. Find one where you are moving just for the sake of the movement, not for any other purpose. Each time I dance Qoya, I marvel at the simplicity of noticing what an emotion feels like in your body and then dancing with it, with both the shadow and the light, shaking out what no longer serves you. The joy of the free dance, enables me to be wildly, truly myself. I feel the lightness in my heart, my soul, my spirit because I get to share this incredible class with other women. Find the movement that brings you the same joy.

Andrea Sherko

❖ **Human well-being requires attention to mind, body, and spirit.** To be wholly well and complete as humans, we must attend to our mental, physical, and spiritual selves. If any one of these aspects of the self is neglected, we remain two-dimensional: we lack substance and depth.

❖ **Music has great power to heal us as individuals.** Listening to music can help us to relax, reflect, and rejuvenate. In addition to providing us with mental and physical benefits, music connects us with Spirit, which optimises our well-being and enables us to live our best possible lives (within the constraints imposed by circumstances beyond our control).

❖ **Spirit (in the form of positive energy) speaks through music, and brings people together.** The power of Spirit, communicating through music, extends beyond individual transformation by bringing people together to form communities for the common good. This is Spirit's most important work, and it is through music that it communicates this message of solidarity to us as the community of humanity.

Dawn Sulley

- **Realign your mind, body and spirit; nurture self-love.** Having healthy spiritual belief gives me a sense of peace and balance among the physical, emotional and social aspects of my life. Being in nature or anywhere outside where there is fresh air will always bring benefits for a person's well-being. Spending time in nature, even if that means a walk around your local park is an effective component of self-care.

- **Accept yourself for who you are.** 'It is during challenging times we find out what we are made of, as that is when we discover the power of our spirit.'(Randi G Fine**)**.

- **Negative thoughts never give you a happy life.** Be amazing today! Never give up anything is possible**.**

Author Bios

From Left:

Top Row: Antoinette Pellegrini, Rosalie Carr, Lesley Lennon, Dawn Sulley.

Bottom Row: Stephen D'Agata, Christine Carmuciano, Andrea Sherko, Liz Reichard.

Antoinette Pellegrini

Antoinette is an Author, Independent Publisher, and Mindset Coach living in a leafy Melbourne suburb in Victoria, Australia.

Antoinette is also a secondary school teacher, working as a teacher for several years before starting a corporate career. She left the corporate world in 2016 to follow her passion for writing and helping others find their voice and achieve their personal goals.

She has raised two amazing young men as a single mother and overcame many hardships and challenges. Antoinette has always been interested in the link between mind, body, and spirit and the critical part the mind plays in relation to overall health, well-being, and achievement of goals. It had been her dream for many years to write books..

Her first book, published in 2017, *Your Thoughts Matter: The Future You Are Creating Starts Now*, contains 25 Reflections and Affirmations on connection and the power of positive thinking and conscious choice. It is designed to empower and inspire the reader to create the life they would like to live.

Antoinette also created an anthology series called, *We Inspire Now*, in which ordinary people share stories of their lives and how they have overcome challenges to follow their passion and live their truth. She has published three books in the series, and this book, *The Spirit Within* is the fourth. She was very honoured that the first three books in the series have all been nominated as finalists for the International Book Awards, at the 2019, 2021 and 2022 American Book Fests.

In 2020, she published her first children's illustrated book, *Sandcastles: A Story About Our Connected World*, which is a story about Bobbie, the sandcastle, and how he discovered that although he was different from the other sandcastles, he was connected to them all. The reader finds out our world is like that too. *Sandcastles* is based on the concepts in her first book, *Your Thoughts Matter*.

As a writing mentor and independent publisher, through her business, We Inspire Now Books, Antoinette has helped people to make their dreams of being published authors a reality. She feels that her journey as an author and publisher has only just begun, and she is looking forward to experiencing every moment that is to come.

www.antoinettepellegrini.com

www.weinspirenowbooks.com

Christine Carmuciano

Christine is a mother of two adult children, each married to wonderful partners. She has been blessed with four grandchildren who constantly fill her life with joy.

A semi-retired woman, she now finds herself wearing many hats since leaving her full-time job in the financial sector.

Since writing her chapter in *A Message To Your Younger Self: What Would You Say?* Christine has completed several courses, including a Diploma in Art Therapy. She now runs workshops and offers a weekly class at a local community house where people of all abilities come together to explore different aspects of themselves in a fun and interactive environment.

A Level 1 Master Reiki healer, she also runs a small practice at home. Her goal is to expand on her spiritual work and continue to help others with these and other modalities, as this is where her passion lies.

Her most treasured times are spent with her family and friends, babysitting her grandchildren and caring for her 98-year-old father. She will jump at any opportunity to travel, which is one of her biggest passions.

As she enters this new decade of her life, her new mantra is to live more simply and joyfully and to shake the chains of dutiful responsibility and past running programmes.

Her goal is to find the carefree Bohemian woman inside of her and live life more freely.

Rosalie Carr

Rosalie's body is that of a 61-year-old, but her mind is still like a teenager's.

She loves to hear other people's life stories and how they have overcome fears, tragedies, grief and disappointments.

Rosalie used to think that she was the only one going through something, but through meeting and talking to many people, she discovered that most people have struggled or are struggling through their own private hell.

Due to a terrible accident, she had when she was 18, Rosalie lost much of her memory, which, in some ways, was a good thing.

Despite her struggles and lifelong depression, her unusual sense of humour is the one thing that has helped her along the way.

Rosalie still sometimes struggles with daily life, and getting out of bed can be a challenge, but her coping skills have improved tenfold.

She loves to get involved in different groups, loves to learn, loves quiz shows, loves napping, socialising, meeting friends for coffee, people-watching, and just discovering new things.

Her motto is. 'Life is full of surprises, so enjoy the ride!!!'

Stephen D'Agata

Born in Melbourne, Australia, on the Feast of Stephen in 1962, Stephen is the fifth of his migrant parents' seven children. His ethnic background covers six countries. An Australian by birth but genealogically Italian and Armenian, his parents were born and raised in Alexandria, Egypt, and his grandparents were born in Turkey, Sicily, and Syria.

In his youth, Stephen balanced his interest in writing and performing against academic achievements in maths and sciences. The technical side eventually won out, and in 1987 he completed a degree in civil engineering. A successful career in water supply, sewerage, and stormwater management, has followed.

In 1992, Stephen met his wife Maria. Almost two years to the day later, they were married and went on to produce a family of three frustratingly fabulous children. Sadly, less than 20 years after their first encounter, Maria lost a six-year-long battle with breast cancer.

Fostering the frustrating fabulosity and artistic talents of his offspring led Stephen to reconnect with his own artistic side. Over the past decade, Stephen has written and performed comedy and prose for open-mic events, performed on stage in amateur theatre productions, and produced online content for YouTube. Links to this content are available at https://stephendagata.wordpress.com/.

His published works include contributions to three anthologies in the *We Inspire Now* series: *Live Your Truth*; *A Message to Your Younger Self*; and now, *The Spirit Within*. His first novel, *Pope Dreams – Pope Peter the Improbable*, is a satirical take on the Papacy and the Catholic Church and was published in December 2022. Available at www.stephendagata.au

Lesley Lennon

Lesley is the proud mother of three adult children, Kara, 32, Grace, 30, and Ben, 27. She is also a grandmother of two, Vinnie, 2 and Sylvie.

As a child, Lesley shared a nomadic lifestyle with her mother, father and two sisters. Lesley's father was a retail store manager, and his job took the family from home to home in Metropolitan and Regional Melbourne and, on occasion, interstate.

When Lesley was 12 years old, her parents settled permanently in a suburb North of Melbourne's CBD. There she completed her High School years, married, and raised her family.

Prior to having children, Lesley began her full-time working life at the State Bank of Victoria. There she was the personal assistant to the Banks Senior Psychologist in the Staff Welfare Department.

When Lesley became a mother in 1990, she initially chose to stay at home. As her three children grew older, she worked in the fitness industry as well as the field of hospitality. At the age of 39, Lesley went to university to obtain her Bachelor of Education at

RMIT University, which she achieved with Distinction.

After many years of teaching, Lesley decided to retire in 2020 to pursue other interests, such as her passion for fashion, writing, exploring her spirituality, travel, and the Arts. Lesley now works casually in an up-market fashion store located in the city of Melbourne.

Liz Reichard

Liz is the founder of Sunranges Qoya.

She found her true calling when she discovered Qoya, a free dance, embodiment class for women, regardless of the gender assigned at birth.

It is designed to get you out of your head and into your body, to feel instead of think. There are no levels in Qoya, and no way to do it wrong. You know you're doing it right because it feels good to you!

Qoya has completely changed Liz's life in all aspects, from her career, to her feelings about her own body, to realising what she can do, while acknowledging what she has already done, and finding new ways to continue exploring the feminine.

She is passionate about bringing Qoya to as many women as she can to help them to also realise how wonderful and powerful they really are.

Through her Qoya classes, Liz promotes women's empowerment, equality, and body neutrality and positivity, to give women a safe space without judgement or shame, to come as they are and leave as more of themselves, to connect with other women in their community, and to raise each other up and empower each other.

If you'd like to know more, head over to www.sunrangesqoya.com.au

Andrea Sherko

Andrea lives in Melbourne, Australia, and has just celebrated (?) her 61st birthday.

Andrea's two main passions are music and animals. She enjoys composing, singing, playing, and listening to a wide range of music, from medieval to pop, and everything in between. She has also enjoyed sharing her home with a variety of furred, feathered, and finned creatures, including cats, rabbits, guinea pigs, canaries, and goldfish. She currently lives with three rather indulged cats: Tosca, Rufus, and Gizmo.

Andrea also loves learning new things. She has tertiary qualifications in Business, Law, Theology, Music, Training and Assessment, and Editing/Proofreading. Although not studying at present, she has an unfulfilled ambition to obtain a Doctorate, hopefully in Music and/or Theology.

Andrea has had a variety of jobs, having worked as a trombone player, music teacher, shop assistant, commercial laundry hand, government investigator and policy officer, lawyer, library assistant, and receptionist at various times, and for varying lengths of time. She is currently caring full-time for her elderly mother, and is taking a break from other paid employment.

As a result of some rather negative experiences, Andrea grew up with an unfavourable view of organised religion. This view persisted for many years, until an incapacitating illness in her early 40s forced her to re-evaluate her life in general, and her spiritual life in particular. This re-evaluation led to many new discoveries, both within and outside the church.

Since 2009 she has been an active participant in the music of the Anglican Church, which has enabled her to combine her love of music with her spiritual quest. Participating in *The Spirit Within* is another step on her path to becoming a more spiritually formed and informed being.

Andrea enjoys writing in a variety of genres, including poetry, short stories, and essays. She is also working on her first novel, *The Saint and the Scribe,* which is based on the life of St Hildegard of Bingen. Samples of Andrea's writings can be viewed on her blog, *Persuasive Words*, which can be found at: https://persuasivewordsnet.blogspot.com/

Dawn Sulley

Dawn was born in the country town of Holbrook, NSW. She was the fourth child in the family, followed by two more brothers. Her parents moved to Wonthaggi in Victoria to be closer to family and friends. When her mother had a breakdown shortly after, Dawn and her siblings were put into a children's home to be cared for until their mother improved. However, this was not to be.

The children were in and out of homes on a regular basis, until all the children were finally placed in the Berry Street Babies Home in Geelong, Victoria. At this point, it was confirmed their mother was in need of further treatment, hence she would be unable to raise her family.

During this time, Dawn and her sister were put up for adoption on the condition that the girls were not to be separated. A few months later, both girls were fostered out to a couple who lived in the country on a small beef cattle farm. Dawn and her sister lived in this family until they were old enough to find employment and leave.

Dawn found herself questioning her identity and tried to find some kind of purpose and meaning to her life. She dealt with issues such as her identity, loss of purpose and unexplained feelings of not belonging. What made such issues spiritual was that they raised questions about the meaning of life, her life in particular. By analysing her spirituality through nightly dreams as a child, she discovered she needed to invest in finding her spirituality through non-religious experiences.

She found connecting with nature, art, meditation and being tuned in to one's self and serving others, gave her a clearer perspective. Practising mindfulness has enabled Dawn to help her mind and body relax and lower her stress levels.

Dawn has found the ability to use her spiritual awareness to express herself creatively. She uses sensory therapy, art, listening to music, writing, appreciating visual and performing arts and reading.

Dawn enjoys engaging in conversations about the meaning of life. She pays attention to the movements in her emotional life when she feels the spirit within herself. This involves looking for hope, compassion, love, trust, and forgiveness. These are important in Dawn's search for meaningful relationships. Dawn has grown spiritually as she learned to nurture these things.

Other Books Published by the Authors in this Anthology

Sandcastles

A Story About Our Connected World

Antoinette Pellegrini (2022)

A story about Bobbie, the sandcastle, and how he discovered that although he was different to the other sandcastles, he was connected to them all. The book includes beautiful illustrations that bring the words to life. Activities are included for children to explore their own connection with the world around them.

Available at all major online retailers and at www.antoinettepellegrini.com

www.weinspirenowbooks.com

Your Thoughts Matter: The Future You Are Creating Starts Now

Antoinette Pellegrini (2017)

Reflections and Affirmations on connection and the power of positive thinking and conscious choice. The series is designed to inspire the reader to create the life they would love to live.

Available at all major online retailers and at:

www.antoinettepellegrini.com

Your Thoughts Matter Reflection Journal and Affirmation Cards

Antoinette Pellegrini (2017)

Accompaniments to the book *Your Thoughts Matter: The Future You Are Creating Starts Now*. The Journal and Affirmation Cards are designed to assist the reader to integrate the learnings into their lives.

Available at:

www.antoinettepellegrini.com

Live Your Truth

Book 1:
We Inspire Now Anthology Series

Created by Antoinette Pellegrini (2018)

Co Author: Stephen D'Agata

Ten authors share their stories about overcoming hardships and difficulties to pursue their goals, discover who they are and live their own truth.

Available at all major online retailers and at
www.antoinettepellegrini.com

www.weinspirenowbooks.com

A Message To Your Younger Self

Book 2
We Inspire Now Anthology Series

Created by Antoinette Pellegrini (2020)

Co-Authors:
Christine Carmuciano and Stephen D'Agata

Ten authors share the messages, words of advice and wisdom they would give their younger selves. It is a book about healing and love - healing the past, taking that healing into the present, and loving the person you were and are today.

Available at all major online retailers and at
www.antoinettepellegrini.com
www.weinspirenowbooks.com

Journey To Me

Book 3
We Inspire Now Anthology Series

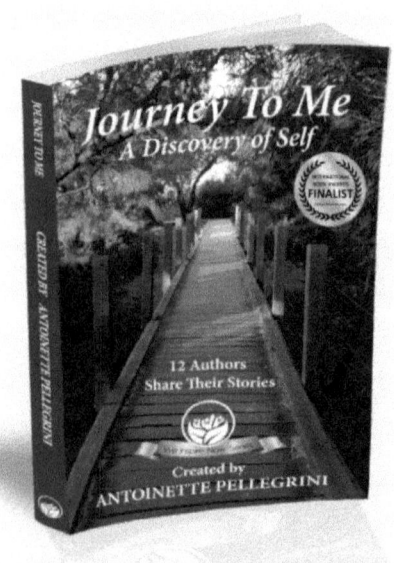

Created by Antoinette Pellegrini (2021)

Co-Authors:
Lesley Lennon and Dawn Sulley

Twelve authors share their personal, inspiring stories of overcoming challenges and difficulties as they explore questions such as 'Who Am I?' and they all have different interpretations.

Available at all major online retailers and at:
www.antoinettepellegrini.com
www.weinspirenowbooks.com

Pope Dreams

Stephen D'Agata

In his first novel, *Pope Dreams,* Stephen D'Agata uses comedy and satire to explore the juxtaposition between the doctrinal Church hierarchy who promote themselves as the conduit to a puppet-master God, and their progressive congregations who recognise a universal God that inextricably connects everyone and everything.

Available at:
www.stephendagata.au

www.ingramcontent.com/pod-product-compliance
Lightning Source LLC
Chambersburg PA
CBHW051537010526
44107CB00064B/2762